Cybersecurity, Hacking, and Espionage – a beginners guide

Author – Abhinav Vaid

Copyright © 2014 by Abhinav Vaid

About the book

Why This Book – While doing testing or whenever there are incidents of hacking, espionage etc. the curiosity of everyone I know keeps growing until it resurfaces after another incident. This book is to capture the entire essence of the subject into one small reference book even for novice or small-time techies.

 –

Who this book is not for - This book is certainly not for Penetration Testers or Security experts as they will find it very basic

This book is for -

– This book is ideal for beginners who are new to security and want to understand high level concepts and do some basic hacking.

A Warning – During the course of writing this book, I had to play with many tools and visit websites which got my computer infected. I was using a Virtual Machine (discussed later in the book), and the viruses could not infect host machine. I could easily fix the VM's by using Malware Bytes anti-virus software. There are some tools that require you to disable antivirus, which is ok in case you have utilities to clean. I found Malware Bytes free version as the most effective.

Conventions Used in the Book - For the purpose of convenience, refer to the table below for various conventions and their intended interpretation.

Convention	Interpretation
	Development - Technical References
	A bookmark
	A sign of Warning
	Web bot - Script to perform automation tasks
	Manual Rating/evaluation
	Future - What Lies Ahead
	Tip

Table of Contents

Table of Figures

Chapter – Computer Hacking – an Introduction

Computer Hacking is a topic of immense debate specially in the recent times due to a variety of reasons. In today's world, anyone who is communicating via a laptop, smartphone, or any similar device is vulnerable to hacking. Simply stated, any act that's targeted to accomplish a task, which one is not authorized to perform is known as hacking. That can be anything including (but not limited to) –

1. Logging into a wireless network, which one is not authorized to

2. Doing a financial transaction in order to get something for free

3. Using someone else's credit card to do a purchase

4. Getting into a Corporate Network for various activities, for example the Sony hack.

5. Getting into Facebook account of others

6. Hacking a Web Server. For example, recent attacks where some hacking group defaced a country's website

7. The most common practices – virus's, spam, malware, Trojans and using Search Engines to exploit vulnerabilities.

Note – The current book covers all the topics with real world examples and the information is shared for informational/non-commercial purposes only

Hacking and Cracking – Differentiation

Hacking is a term often confused by many for example, there are people who call hacking as a technique to do something really geek, which is often hard to accomplish as a normal practice or not known to a common end user. An example could be using Gmail to send SMS or to make a phone call for free.

Simply stated, the examples are targeted for Good Intentions

Cracking is typically coined towards the unethical practices, which are often due to bad/evil Intentions. Although lately, hacking term is often being used for evil intentions and cracking.

Types of Hackers

A hacker is someone who likes to tinker with electronics or computer systems. Hackers like to explore and learn how computer systems work, finding ways to make them do what they do better, or do things they weren't intended to do. Typically, there are three types of hackers –

Intent/Goal Driven Hackers -

White Hat – These are considered the good guys. White hat hackers don't use their skills for illegal purposes. They usually become Computer Security experts and help protect people from the Black Hats. It is not uncommon to see former back hat hackers to get employed in Security Organizations. In fact, in many countries, cyber criminals have been known to help Government agencies to solve cybercrime cases.

Grey Hat – Undefined category as it lies in between White Hat and Black Hat and there are no governing bodies/established rules and/or processes. They do not have legitimate permission to hack protected systems and do it either for fun or to detect security vulnerabilities. The intent is typically to alert the legitimate users about the underlying flaws so that they can be fixed.

Black Hat – These are considered the bad guys. Black hat hackers usually use their skills maliciously for personal gain. They are the people that hack banks, steal credit cards, deface websites etc. They exploit vulnerabilities to gain access to the systems followed by obtaining or destroying information and take control of the systems till the unethical objectives are achieved.

Skill based Hackers -

Script kiddies – the term is pretty much based on the dictionary i.e., lesser skilled/kids. There is, however, another dimension to it. These hackers either due to lack of knowledge or with an urge to cut corners have at times proven to be most fatal.

Intermediate hackers – refer to the people who have been there for a while and understand the domain and technology that surrounds around hacking. They are capable to understand existing code, tools, technologies and equally capable to use the technology with little modifications.

Elite Hackers – refers to the elite crowd, who know it all. They have created Tools, Technologies, Scripts etc. and contribute significantly in the world of hacking.

What does it take to become a hacker?

As many believe, it is not that difficult to become a hacker, but it requires a lot of determination to remain focused while you do the hard work and research. However, retaining focus on what you want to accomplish could be far easier than trying to learn everything. For example, in case you only intend to get into Facebook account, or a corporate network could be much easier than get overwhelmed by the doors that start opening once you start getting the success. In case you really want to become a hacker, following skills are required:

1. Operating Systems – although Microsoft Windows is the most popular operating system, Linux is not that hard either. Kali distribution is very popular and comes integrated with a lot of penetration testing tools. It is also a GUI based and user friendly.

2. **Computer Basics** - basic understanding of computer is essential to start with for example, registry, directory structure etc.

3. **Virtualization** - **knowledge** of virtualization tools like Virtual box and VMWare helps a lot spinning of your own VM for hacking. It saves your own machine from getting effected.

4. **Scripting** – knowledge of scripting helps a lot while hacking. Programming language like Python is relatively easy and can be learnt quickly.

5. **Networking** – basic networking skills like IP addressing, DNS, TCP/IP etc. provide a great help in what's happening behind the scenes. Computers are connected via LAN (Local Area Network) and WAN (Wide Area Network). Ethernet cables are typically used in Local Area Network and WAN's are connected via routers and Access points. For small areas Wi-Fi has become very popular and that's another reason it's one of the favorites among hackers. Small time hackers just crack the passwords to do free browsing and the more seasoned hackers use other person's network to perform malicious activities.

6. **Database** – knowledge of SQL helps in hacking and penetration testing. SQL injection is a very popular technique used by hackers. Knowledge of Oracle and SQL Server will also aid you in understanding behind the scene concepts.

Getting Started in Hacking -

There are various aspects that need to be considered before taking up hacking as a passion and or profession. Since the World Wide Web drives everything, the most basic requirement is understanding how html language works. And then keep diving based on the what one intends to accomplish by hacking.

The Pulse of Hacking – nuts and bolts that no one wants you to know?

Who Creates the Virus's – This is a lesser-known fact about the Security Organizations that spread virus's and then offer updates to clean them. Alternatively, there are many anti-virus companies that release virus's in case the subscription is not extended. In case you really want to create a test virus and then clean it, go to www.eicar.com. This is useful in case you want to test the effectiveness of anti-virus engine.

Who Creates Spam – Marketing Professionals, Organizations, and spammers (for malicious or research purposes). They are becoming more multi-talented as well rather than just offering bot networks for DDoS attacks or Spam you can also hire them to get stolen credit card info, PayPal accounts, bank accounts for credit references, to set up a secure VPN and much more

Social Aspects –

Facebook, Instagram, and other social media platforms have become a profession of many. The End users are not informed enough and that creates further complications. Social engineering has been around for a while now, so it is the right time to address the nuisances. The Social Engineering Vulnerability Evaluation and Recommendation (SEVER) Project is one way to help.

The Government Aspects –

The laws governing the cyber space are either not there or still in the process of evolution. That makes it an easy game for hackers.

The Business Aspects –

It is quite unfortunate that many Organizations on the Social Media platforms seem to be exploiting the platform. It was very common to see virus's, adware, and spam on social media. It is good to see Facebook hiring web content evaluators who evaluate and get the spam removed.

The 7 layers of Network – The Core

An end user does not know what lies underneath while he is working on an application. For example, a user enters a URL into a web browser. The browser looks up the IP address for the domain name (for example, google.com) via DNS. The browser sends a HTTP request to the server. The server sends back a HTTP response. The application layer (topmost layer) provides full end-user access to a variety of shared network services for data flow. This layer has many responsibilities, including error handling and recovery, data flow over a network and full network flow. It is also used to develop network-based applications. Overall the other hand, there are 7 layers of network from which the data has to pass through before it reaches the end user. All the 7 layers are built on a set of standards. One layer only communicates with the next and it becomes difficult to predict how an application will behave based on real world/live network. Each and every layer is extremely complex and is built on standards laid down by the governing bodies. The seven layers of network also known as OSI reference model are typically divided into two categories: upper layers (layers 4 through 7) and lower layers (layers 1 through 3). As you can determine from the example of displayed in Figure 2, the OSI model provides a service that allows information to flow smoothly from one layer to another.

There remain vulnerabilities at every layer and anyone, with reasonable level of understanding with some research can try hitting the application from every layer.

The best example is the Physical layer (geeks call it **PHI** layer) and refers to the physical connection (for example the Ethernet cable socket, that connects a computer/laptop with the network). This was one of the safest and the only area, where security practitioners used to be very confident about security and would typically ignore. Exploiting it would require physically tampering the connection and one does not need anything except a camera, which captures that no one is tampering the connection.

But now, the world has transitioned to 11n and we see WIFI everywhere right from our homes to Airports, and Organizations, public hotspots and so on. With every Organization trying to make it quick shipment to the market missed out many aspects of security. Based on the benefits that it offers, the transition was so quick that before anyone could realize, the WLAN had already penetrated the world. With zillions of vulnerabilities already live, it was quite impossible to do a backtrack and the world continued to live with the flaws. No one talks about it because whistle blowers (who are the part of the Organizations) are severely punished, and the Governments are not informed enough to make the right choices. Yes, there is an encouraging part because Security practices are constantly being updated, new patches being added.

There was a time, when anyone could just go to the Airport and see open WLAN ports waiting for everyone to connect, which is no longer true. At a high level, here is what happens when a user clicks a query on browser and gets the results. Please refer to figure 1 that displays the background process of what happens when an end user triggers a search and receives back the results:

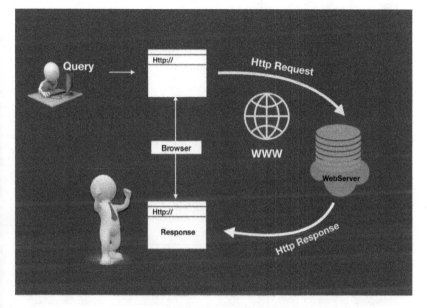

Figure 1 - Request and Response Query

Technically all Wireless LANs operate on the Physical and Data Link layers, layers 1 and 2. All Wi-Fi systems use these layers to format data and control the data to conform with 802.11 standards. Medium arbitration-controlling when the Access Point can access the medium and transmit or receive data-is done at these two layers.

As discussed earlier, the International Standards Organization (ISO) developed the Open Systems Interconnection (OSI) model. It divides network communication into seven layers. In this model, layers 1-4 are considered the lower layers, and mostly concern themselves with moving data around.

The 7 layers of network is called an OSI model and is explained in Figure 2 below –

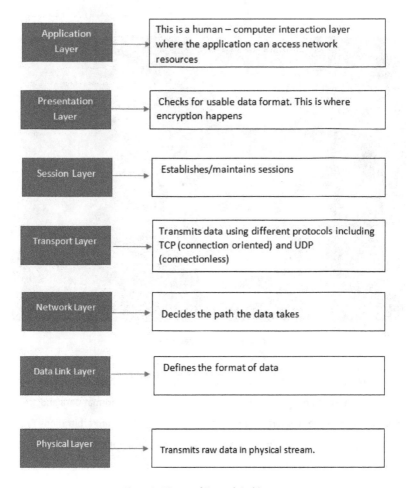

Figure 2 - 7 Layers of Network Architecture

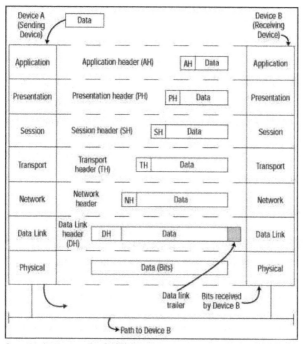

Figure 2.2 End user header and trailer flow.

Figure 3 - - How data processes

Underlying Software Architecture –

There are 2 types of common architectures in the world of web -

Unix/Linux based – Apache Server with a database (Oracle etc.) with php (scripting language)

Microsoft Windows – IIS based with a sql database and asp.net as the front end language

The Operating Systems –

Microsoft Windows – Microsoft does a pretty good job in fixing vulnerabilities but is the most targeted Operating System due to widest market penetration. Most of the virus's, malware etc. target Microsoft Windows. Unlike to (as many believe), used to be the most vulnerable Operating System ironically due to its design. Charles Petzold (the most acclaimed author of Windows) puts it like this – *Windows is extremely complicated system, which has put a programming layer on top of it (which is called an API), which merely hides this complexity. One day, sooner or later, this complexity is going to come out and bite you right on the leg.*

Since Windows has the widest market penetration and most vulnerable, most of the content in the current book has been compiled on Windows.

MAC OSX – by Apple is extremely popular and secure.

Linux – although not popular, but the best Operating System for hackers. It comes with a variety of flavors/distributions and Kali Linux is the most popular one.

The Clients – Servers, Computers, Tablets, Phablets, and Smartphones -

Can be anything that has a browser and connected to Internet for example a mobile phone (android/iOS), a tablet, or a laptop/desktop computer

The handshaking Protocols -

HTTP – the most common protocol to access internet but least secured. There was a time when majority of the sites used HTTP protocol, but the trend has changed, and sites have migrated towards https which is more secured.

HTTPS – the secured (encrypted protocol) typically used in Banking and Financial Transaction Sites. Other sites are also transitioning towards https due to enhanced security.

FTP – File Transfer Protocol – typically used by Webmaster for managing a web site. This is an often overlooked by many Organizations and make the network vulnerable to attacks.

SFTP - Secure File Transfer Protocol (SFTP) is a secure version of File Transfer Protocol (FTP), which facilitates data access and data transfer over a Secure Shell (SSH) data stream. It is part of the SSH Protocol.

The browsers -

Internet Explorer – The most popular web browser by Microsoft and the most vulnerable. Internet Explorer is the single most actively exploited piece of software on most computers. A majority of computer spyware and adware makes its way onto your computer through Internet Explorer's security holes. This is largely because Internet Explorer was designed to grant websites control over end user's computer, and malicious websites could easily abuse this power, automatically installing programs and viruses onto target computer without end user's consent. Once a target computer is hit with a spyware or adware attack, Microsoft says the only solution may be to dump your system and start from scratch.

Firefox – The most secure, comes with some extremely valuable add-ons, for example -

- **Live headers**

- **Firefox developer tools**

Google Chrome – although latest but one of the most popular browser released by Google. Fast but invasive, tracks pretty much everything and at times does not even seek permission. No wonder, not much popularity in the hackers' community.

Note - When it comes to privacy and cybersecurity, new research suggests that Firefox is definitely the most secure browser. The German Federal Office for

Information Security (BSI) tested Mozilla Firefox 68 (ESR), Google Chrome 76, Microsoft Internet Explorer 11, and Microsoft Edge 44 to determine the most secure browser.

Two Uncommon browsers – two browsers that I personally use a lot include Tor and I2P. They are discussed in detail during the later part of the book.

Tor - Simplest browser for covering the tracks. Use Tor for covering the online activity, at least as a beginner.

I2P – one of the best browsers to remain anonymous on Internet

Chapter – Using Search Engines to Hack

The Title of the chapter might look deceiving, but it is not. Although you do get a prompt that the Tool should be used only for the Information purpose only.

Using Google Tool –

1. In order to download the tool, go to www.google.com/p/googlehacks

2. Install the Tool

3. Invoke the Tool.

4. Click hack and hit the Search button

Figure 4 - Using Google Research Tools to Hack

A simple query of hack with the default configuration displays the results as shown in the Figure 5. Use the creativity to find whatever you need and in whatever format.

Using Google Browser to hack

There is no limit on how far you can reach with Google's own search engine, be it hacking, cracking and so on. Let's start –

1. Invoke the browser

2. Type the command – "filetype:log inurl:"password.log" in the search field and hit the return key

3. The Search Engine Results Page gets displayed with real world passwords and related information

Note – This is a dangerous trick especially while using Google for similar tasks. There is really nothing hidden when you work on the browser. Whatever activity you do is tracked specially by Organizations like Microsoft and Google.

Figure 6 - Using Google to find passwords for hacking

For the sake of demonstration, only one example of Google (Figure 6) has been covered in the current book.

Using Microsoft Bing to Hack

On the similar lines of Google example, any search engine can be used as long as you know the right strings to search.

1. Invoke a browser

2. Navigate to www.bing.com

3. In the search field, enter a search string based on what you look forward to accomplish. For example, enter a query filetype:pdf "Host Vulnerability Summary Report" "Assessment Report and hit the return key.

4. Search Engine Results Page will get displayed (Refer to Figure 7)

5. You will see Vulnerability Summary Reports in Search Engine Results page. Combining the search string with a site name you want to target will reveal loopholes that can be used for hacking the target web site.

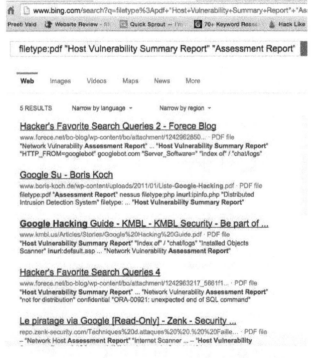

Figure 7 - - Finding Network Vulnerability using Microsoft Bing

Using DuckDuckGo Search Engine

DuckDuckGo has been hitting the charts lately and has become a search engine of choice among the people who want to remain anonymous. This browser is one of the products being promoted by large communities who believe in Internet anonymity. It is non-invasive and does not track every activity. That said, we would be running a few commands to see how far the creativity of playing with operators can take you.

1. To start with Invoke the Browser.

2. Downloading eBooks for free without using credit card. Try this query "inurl:thanks for payment intitle:click here to download"

3. Watching someone's bedroom and or security cameras for free. Type the query "inurl view index shtml bedroom" and hit the return key

4. The Search Engine Results Page shows up (Figure 9)

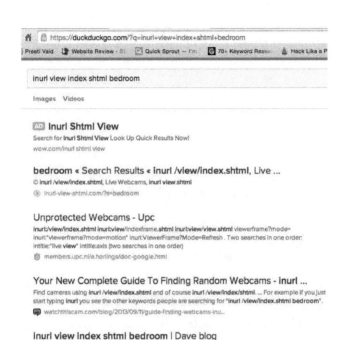

Figure 8 - Watching what's happening in the bedrooms of others

5. Want to go nastier, Click the Images Button on Figure 8 and you will get a shock (Figure 9)

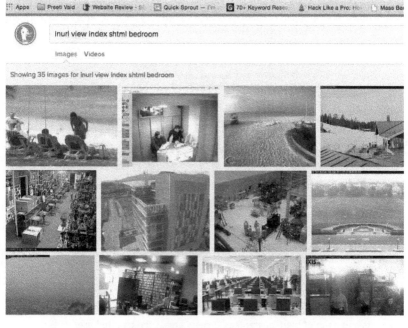

Figure 9 - bedroom information

Finding Facebook Passwords – the lethal way

1. Invoke the browser

2. Type the command "intitle:"Index of" passwords modified" and hit the return key.

3. SERP (Search Engine Results Page) is displayed with the passwords that were recently modified.

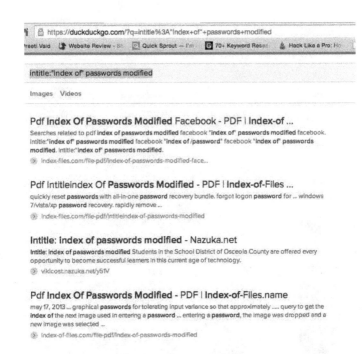

Figure 10 - Latest Facebook Passwords

Other Ways to Hack Facebook – There are more than 10 ways to hack Facebook accounts and none of them guarantees success unless the targeted user does a mistake for example, clicking a link or an attachment. One of the most reliable tool is Facebook Hacker Pro 2.8.9 Crack. The links keep changing and a simple google search will reveal the URL to download.

The software will prompt you to disable the windows defender or other Anti-Virus application. Ensure to re-enable the application and run a full system scan after you are done with hacking Facebook account.

Getting Nastier – Finding web to see what's being tried to hack

Ever wondered what sites hackers are currently being targeted, how many hackers are trying and from what part of the world…. It's all there!

A little creativity and some political information can lead to monstrous information using the browser. A few examples -

Pakistan Sites

Hackers with a little creativity target Pakistan Government sites and some knowledge of google operators reveals it all.

1. Invoke the browser
2. Go to Google.com
3. Type "inurl /admi" and stop. Notice the auto suggestions that are cropping up. Now these are the popular searches people are searching to get the admin credentials of Pakistani web sites. It is Google's auto complete feature that gives the drop down with suggestions based on high volume of these types of queries.

Notice that Pakistan site's administrative login information is being searched for. Refer to Figure 11

✓ Google's auto complete feature can give great inputs to what sites are being targeted for hacking/malicious purposes

✓ Getting into Google's Webmaster's account can get you the numbers etc.

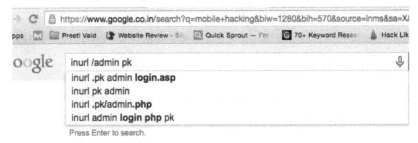

Figure 11 - Pakistan sites – being tried to hack

Hacking Windows Passwords

Windows to Windows hacking – Let us do an experiment to hack one Windows Machine from another one.

1. Security Accounts Manager (SAM) – is a default file used in Microsoft Windows for storing encrypted passwords.

2. The SAM is located in C:\Windows\system32\config

3. Two utilities are needed before you can start hacking. The Utilities (Figure 12) are available under Open Source GPL License -

    I. Pwdump3 and

    II. Pwdump3e

4. Install the Utilities

5. Grab the Hashes using Pwdump3

Note - Check your OS as there are different utilities for different versions of windows.

Reference - https://www.openwall.com/passwords/windows-pwdump

pwdump3 and pwdump3e by Phil Staubs and Erik Hjelmstad of PoliVec, Inc.
Windows NT/2000, free (GPL v2)
Download local copies of pwdump3 version 2 (87 KB) and pwdump3e (217 KB)

pwdump3 enhances the existing pwdump and pwdump2 programs developed by Jeremy Allison and Todd Sabin, respectively. pwdump3 works across the network and whether or not SYSKEY is enabled. Like the previous pwdump utilities, pwdump3 does not represent a new exploit since administrative privileges are still required on the remote system. One of the largest improvements with pwdump3 over pwdump2 is that it allows network administrators to retrieve hashes from a remote NT system.

pwdump3e provides enhanced protection of the password hash information by encrypting the data before it is passed across the network. It uses Diffie-Hellman key agreement to generate a shared key that is not passed across the network, and employs the Windows Crypto API to protect the hashes.

Figure 12 - Using pwdump

6. Pwdump3 is able to grab the encrypted passwords. We need to further crack them with another password cracking tool. So, let's grab that SAM

file with pwdump3

7. Grab the Hashes

8. Open a command prompt and navigate to -

   C:/abhinav/Desktop/pwdump3 mylinux hashdumpfile.txt

9. Click the Return key

10. The Utility pwdump3 will grab the password hashes and save them inside the file called "**hashdumpfile.txt**".

11. The first part is over, and we have successfully grabbed the encrypted passwords (hashes). The next step is to decrypt.

Using Cain & Abel -

Cain & Abel is a password recovery tool for Microsoft Operating Systems. It allows easy recovery of various kinds of passwords by sniffing the network, cracking encrypted passwords using Dictionary, Brute-Force and Cryptanalysis attacks, recording VoIP conversations, decoding scrambled passwords, recovering wireless network keys, revealing password boxes, uncovering cached passwords and analyzing routing protocols. Now lets use Cain & Abel to decrypt passwords.

Final Stage – Lets Crack the Passwords

1. Invoke the Tool (refer to Figure 15)
2. Click the "Cracker" tab (4th from either side).
3. Enter Cain and Abel the password hashes to crack.
4. Select the second radio button – "Import Hashes from a text file.
5. Select the encrypted file that was generated earlier.
6. A Using Dictionary Attacks for Password Cracking dialog box as displayed in Figure 15 will be displayed.

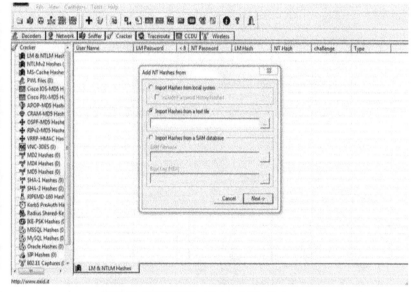

Figure 13 - Cracking Windows Passwords Using Hash

You have option to use any of the attack for the options displayed in the Figure 14

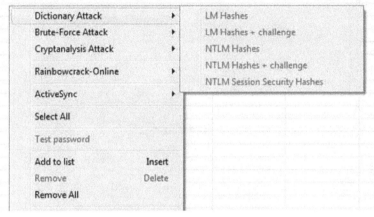

Figure 14 - Using Dictionary Attacks for Password Cracking

8. Navigating to Cain folder will reveal a folder by the name of "Wordlist."
9. Use your preferred option. You Will feel invincible – I bet

Using different Techniques for Hacking Passwords -

Metasploit and pwdump3

In the previous section, we discussed about cracking windows password using pwdump3 but in that case we assumed physical access to the computer. What in case you don't have the physical access? This can be accomplished using Metasploit.

Using Dictionary Attacks

A dictionary attack is when a text file full of commonly used passwords, or a list of every word from the dictionary is used against a password database. Strong passwords usually aren't vulnerable to this kind of attack.

One of the best tool to do dictionary attack is Brutus, but there is a limitation that it works only on Windows and preferred choice to hit the server via FTP instead of http.

Using Rainbow Tables

A Rainbow table is a huge pre-computed list of hash values for every possible combination of characters. A password hash is a password that has gone through a mathematical algorithm that transformed it into something absolutely foreign. A hash is a one- w a y encryption so once a password is hashed there is no way to get the original string from the hashed string. A very common hashing algorithm used as security to store passwords in website databases is MD5.

Let's say you are registering for a website. You put in a username and password. Now when you submit, the password goes through the MD5 algorithm and the outcome hash is stored in a database. Now since you can't get the password from the hash, you may be wondering how they know if the password is right when you login. Well when you login and submit the username and password, a script takes the password and runs it through the md5 algorithm. The outcome hash is compared to the hash stored in the database. If they are the same, you are admitted.

If I were to run the word "**cheese**" through the md5 algorithm, the outcome would be **fea0f1f6fede90bd0a925b4194deac11**. Having huge tables of every possible character combination hashed is a much better alternative to brute-force cracking. Once the rainbow tables are created, cracking the password is a hundred times faster than brute-forcing it.

Cracking Windows Passwords Using Ophcrack –

This is one of the most popular utilities to crack Windows passwords. Ophcrack operates only on Microsoft Windows due to a design flaw in Microsoft Windows. Rainbow Tables, a hacking technique is used to crack the passwords using Ophcrack.

Microsoft Windows does not store passwords in plain text. In order to ensure the security of Operating System, passwords are converted and stored in encrypted form. Microsoft Windows supports a variety of hashes and Lan Manager is one of them. According the algorithm, if the password is longer than seven characters, it is broken into seven chunks of characters. The characters are further converted into Upper Case and finally encrypted with DES. Since the Password is Upper Case and broken into smaller chunks, the number of password combinations gets reduced. The passwords are stored in a variety of places including -

C:\WINDOWS\system32\config\SAM

Registry - HKEY_LOCAL_MACHINE\SAM where it is also locked for all users

Next Step is to grab the hashes. Some popular techniques include -

Using Windows - PWDUMP program that comes with Ophcrack to trick the registry into giving up the hashes.

Using Linux – use the preconfigured CD with Linux distribution and copy the SAM file to a usb disk

Let's start hacking -

1. Download and Install Ophcrack.

2. Installer will prompt for the components (Refer to Figure 15)

3. For the purpose of brevity, we will just install the first component.

4. Continue with Installation till you get a prompt to download Rainbow Tables.

5. Download Rainbow Tables.

Install Rainbow Tables.

After the completion of installation, Invoke the browser and go to Ophcrack

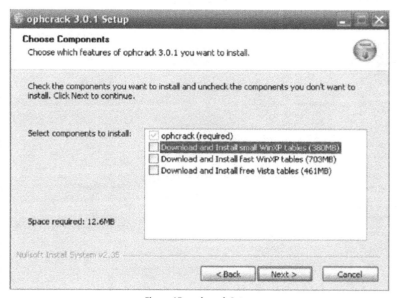

Figure 15 - ophcrack Setup

website.

6. Navigate to Rainbow Tables.

7. Choose the Table based on the machine configuration.

8. Invoke ophcrack and click on tables.

9. Select the table you downloaded and click Install to locate the file on the computer. Hit the Return key.

10. Running PWDUMP to obtain the password hashes

11. Disable the scanners. This is a requirement otherwise the Anti-Virus engine will block the program.

12. Click Load and select Local SAM.

13. The Password Hashes will be displayed. Refer to Figure 16

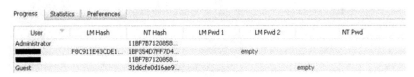

User	LM Hash	NT Hash	LM Pwd 1	LM Pwd 2	NT Pwd
Administrator		11BF7B7120858...			
▮▮▮▮▮	F8C911E43CDE1...	1BF354D7FF7D4...		empty	
Guest		11BF7B7120858...			
		31d6cfe0d16ae9...			empty

Figure 16 - Password Hashes of all the Users in the System

Hit the Crack button.

The cracking program starts.

Finally, once the passwords have been cracked, a confirmation dialog box will get displayed (refer to Figure 17)

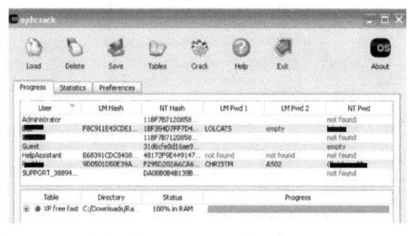

Figure 17 - Confirmation of Cracked accounts

Chapter - Hacking the World Wide Web

Post the Web 2.0 era, most websites are dynamic and allow the users to interact with the content. Many of the web applications that run these dynamic websites have security flaws. In this chapter, we will discuss some of the most popular forms of attacks against web applications.

Using Cross Site Scripting

Cross-site scripting (XSS) occurs when a user is able to inject malicious code into a webpage, which results in unpredictable results. XSS attacks are very popular and some of the biggest websites have been affected by them right from FBI, Ebay, Apple, Microsoft, and Sony, to Official Government Sites. The typical entry points for this kind of attacks include -

        a. Search Engines

        b. Login Forms

        c. Comment Fields

There are three types of XSS attacks:

1. **Local Attacks** – Local XSS attacks are very rare but extremely hard to manage. This attack looks for an exploit in and around browser vulnerabilities. This type of attack can allow a hacker to install works, backdoors, and viruses etc.

2. **Non-Persistent Attacks** – these are very common and frequent but not capable enough to do any significant damage. Non-persistent attacks occur when (a scripting language that is used for client-side web development) or HTML is inserted into a variable, which causes the output (the user sees) to be changed. Non-persistent attacks are only

activated when the user visits the URL that's been put together by the hacker.

3. **Persistent Attacks** – Persistent attacks are usually used against web applications like guest books, forums, and other social media platforms. Some of the tasks the hacker can perform include -

      a. Defacing websites

      b. Stealing cookies

      c. Spreading Worms

Detecting XSS Vulnerabilities –

As Security Practitioners/Testers, these are some of the steps that we perform during Vulnerability Assessment -

1. Enter a unique word in the search field and hit enter, in case the word appears in on the next page, it is vulnerable.

2. Insert HTML code and search for **<h1>hi</h1>**, and if the same word pops up, the site is vulnerable

3. JavaScript - Search for **<script>alert("hi");</script>** , if the word "hi" pops up in a popup box, the site is vulnerable. Refer to Figure 18

Figure 18 - Java Script Vulnerability

I tried using **<script>alert("hi");</script>** on my personal website and got the confirmation that the command is "Not Acceptable". This confirmed that my site is properly patched and not vulnerable. Refer to the screen capture displayed in Figure 19:

Not Acceptable!

An appropriate representation of the requested resource could not be found on this server. This error was generated by Mod_Security.

Figure 19 - Java Script Vulnerability Test

Phishing Attacks

JavaScript is very popular for conducting Phishing attacks. Let's try some examples,

1. If a hacker wants to phish passwords from www.testingrecipes.in. All it takes to know is to find a vulnerability in the website and crafting a link to the actual website that can redirect it to phishing site.

2. In the above example, inserting a JavaScript code in the search translates like this -

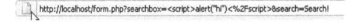

http://localhost/form.php?searchbox=<script>alert("hi")<%2Fscript>&search=Search!

✓ For the purpose of demonstration, the example is implemented on a local copy (localhost), instead of Production Site.

✓ Tip – the code typed to search box was passed to the "search box" variable instead

3. Select all the text and replace it with the following JavaScript code- <script>window.location = "http://targeted_phishing_site.com"</script

4. Any user clicking on the legitimate link will now get navigated to the redirected site (added in point 3)

Using FootPrints

This is the first step any hacker performs. As the name suggests, FootPrinting is finding information about the potential targeted hacking site. Here is a high-level list of FootPrint steps -

1. In order to find information on the target site, for example, in order to hack www.testingrecipes.in, a simple Google query will give the results or the link to the target web site

2. Using a command prompt, ping the web site and it will reply along with the IP address and the status of the site (whether it is accessible/live or not).

3. The IP address of target web site is displayed in Figure 20.

```
●●●                         abhinavvaid — ping — 80×24
              GIMP      screencapture                        ping
64 bytes from 208.91.198.242: icmp_seq=37 ttl=115 time=326.886 ms
64 bytes from 208.91.198.242: icmp_seq=38 ttl=115 time=309.670 ms
64 bytes from 208.91.198.242: icmp_seq=39 ttl=115 time=316.616 ms
64 bytes from 208.91.198.242: icmp_seq=40 ttl=115 time=311.355 ms
64 bytes from 208.91.198.242: icmp_seq=41 ttl=115 time=306.504 ms
64 bytes from 208.91.198.242: icmp_seq=42 ttl=115 time=323.826 ms
64 bytes from 208.91.198.242: icmp_seq=43 ttl=115 time=320.841 ms
64 bytes from 208.91.198.242: icmp_seq=44 ttl=115 time=324.502 ms
64 bytes from 208.91.198.242: icmp_seq=45 ttl=115 time=310.495 ms
64 bytes from 208.91.198.242: icmp_seq=46 ttl=115 time=317.548 ms
64 bytes from 208.91.198.242: icmp_seq=47 ttl=115 time=307.489 ms
64 bytes from 208.91.198.242: icmp_seq=48 ttl=115 time=308.873 ms
64 bytes from 208.91.198.242: icmp_seq=49 ttl=115 time=318.599 ms
64 bytes from 208.91.198.242: icmp_seq=50 ttl=115 time=312.862 ms
64 bytes from 208.91.198.242: icmp_seq=51 ttl=115 time=304.906 ms
64 bytes from 208.91.198.242: icmp_seq=52 ttl=115 time=316.773 ms
64 bytes from 208.91.198.242: icmp_seq=53 ttl=115 time=317.654 ms
64 bytes from 208.91.198.242: icmp_seq=54 ttl=115 time=315.803 ms
64 bytes from 208.91.198.242: icmp_seq=55 ttl=115 time=305.474 ms
64 bytes from 208.91.198.242: icmp_seq=56 ttl=115 time=316.709 ms
64 bytes from 208.91.198.242: icmp_seq=57 ttl=115 time=306.970 ms
64 bytes from 208.91.198.242: icmp_seq=58 ttl=115 time=317.662 ms
64 bytes from 208.91.198.242: icmp_seq=59 ttl=115 time=307.994 ms
```

Figure 20 - Ping Results - Target Website

Navigate to http://whois.domaintools.com/testingrecipes.in **and see the results**

(Figure 21). It says pretty much everything.

Figure 21 - Ping Results - Target Website

4. As discussed in the power of Search Engines earlier, the same creativity can be used here as well. For example, a hacker could search a website through Google by searching "site:www.the-target-site.com" this will display every page that Google has of the website.

5. Power of Robots.txt – Robots.txt was implemented to ensure that search engine crawlers do not invade the websites and the folders specified in this file are not supposed to be crawled by the bots. But try Google "inurl:robots.txt this would look for a page called robots.txt. If a site has the file "robots.txt", it displays all the directories and pages on the website that they wish to keep anonymous from the search engine spiders. No wonder

why hacks are frequent!

Using Penetration Testing

Penetration Testing also known as Pen Testing is one of the jobs that Security Testers do. Penetration Testers are employed to do testing of in-house applications or web sites. It is indeed interesting to see that a practice of hiring Penetration testers came up as a reactive measure instead of what it should have been there at the first place.

There are variety of ways in which Penetration Testing and Vulnerability assessment is done using various tools and scripting languages. Let's do some basic hands on to see the possibilities.

Using PHP to hack

PHP is the most basic and the most popular scripting language on the web. No wonder, its exploits are also common. PHP exploit code usually starts with **<?php** and ends in **?>** .

Example - Let's say a hacker wanted to do some temporary damage to a server running **FTP Server**. If he was to search milw0rm he would come up with the following DOS exploit: http://www.testingrecipes.com/exploits/2901 and run it against the server. Below are the steps the hacker would take.

1. Install PHP.

2. Install WAMP - a free web server that can be used in Linux/Windows Environment. Mac equivalent of WAMP is MAMP (being used in the current example).

3. Copy the code and paste the PHP exploit into notepad or any

equivalent editor.

4. Save the file as "**exploit.php**".

A MAMP Server looks as the one displayed in Figure 22. Understanding web servers is relatively straightforward due to the wizard driven (GUI based applications).

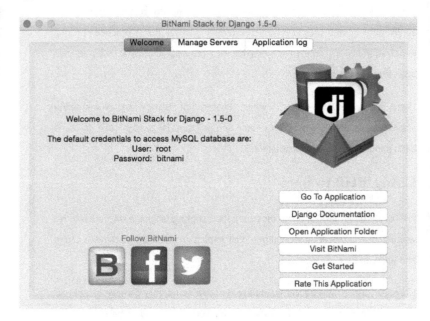

Figure 22 - Using BitNami Stack

5. On the browser it looks like –

$address = gethostbyname('192.168.1.100');

6. Save the file in PHP directory

7. Navigate to the Application folder and invoke Django as displayed in the

Figure 22

8. Invoke the Terminal

9. Navigate to PHP directory

```
● ● ●                    🏠 abhinavvaid — use_djangostack — bash — 80×24
Last login: Mon Jan 19 21:30:37 on ttys001
Abhinavs-MacBook-Pro:~ abhinavvaid$ /Applications/BitNamiStackForDjango.app/Cont
ents/Resources/app/use_djangostack ; exit;
bash-3.2$ ▓
```

Figure 23 - Terminal screen

Time to HACK -

4. Type "php exploit.php" and hit enter. Bingo, here you go.

```
●  ●  ●              ⌂ abhinavvaid — use_djangostack — bash — 80×16
   51  cd diago
   52  ls
   53  cd django
   54  ls
   55  cd scripts
   56  ls
   57  exploit.php
   58  ls
   59  history
bash-3.2$ cd\
> ls
bash: cdls: command not found
bash-3.2$ pwd
/Users/abhinavvaid/Library/Containers/com.bitnami.django/Data/app/apps/django/sc
ripts
bash-3.2$ exploit.php█
```

Figure 24 - Run Exploit

Tip – It is natural to run into small code related issues time and again. A little research over Google goes a long way.

DoS attack will get triggered on the Targeted site – **WEBSITE HACKED**

Crashing your company's web site using DoS/DDoS

Jokes apart, one of my cousin brought down the website of his high school. Fortunately, he was not booted off and just issued a warning. This is one of the favorite among script kiddies since it is very easy to implement. Back in time DOS (Denial of Service) was a very popular but now DDoS (Distributed Denial of Service) is the latest.

What is DoS?

Denial of Service or DoS is an attack meant to shut down a machine/network/website, making it inaccessible to the intended users. DoS attacks accomplish this by flooding the target with traffic.

What is DDoS?

The objective of DDoS is to crash a website. In technical terms, it is used to bring down a website by pushing it with traffic that it is unable to process. While DOS was popular using single computer, but DDoS uses multiple attackers to flood the target website.

Quantifying the magnitude of DDoS attack

According to this securelist.com, 82% of attacks last less than 4 hours. According to Sans.org, 34% clock in at between 100 MB's to 1 GB's, and only 5.3% exceed the 10 GB/s mark.

A 1 GB/s denial-of-service attack is strong enough to take down most of the websites out there, since their data hosting simply doesn't offer enough bandwidth to keep the site online. One of the most popular attack was done by Mirai botnet that impacted the DNS server and cascaded to taking down Redditt and Twitter temporarily.

Hackers or competitors are known to use it against competitors. Some government websites are also taken down using DDoS. Script kiddies have known to test their skills or just have fun.

DDoS Tools and Utilities

Back in time of DOS, ping of death was a common mechanism to bring down a website but now the Servers are hosted on powerful infrastructure with a lot of security. This makes DDoS a little tricky. There are many tools available to generate the traffic. Alternatively, if you get associated with a group such as Anonymous it makes it a breeze to take their help. They are known to attack with uses flooding the targeted website being generated from across the globe. Below is the list of some of the most popular tools to do DDoS:

1. OWASP DOS HTTP POST
2. Tor's Hammer
3. Low Orbit Ion Cannon
4. XOIC
5. DDOSIM – Layer 7 DDoS Simulator
6. R-U-Dead-Yet.

7. GoldenEye HTTP Denial of Service Tool

How to DDoS an IP using Command Prompt

As discussed earlier, one of the basic attack is called the "ping of death", and uses the Command Prompt to flood an Internet Protocol address with data packets.

Because of its small scale and basic nature, ping of death attacks usually works best against smaller targets. For instance, the attacker can target:

a)   A single computer. However, in order for this to be successful, the malicious hacker must first find out the IP address of the device.

b)   A wireless router. Flooding the router with data packets will prevent it from sending out Internet traffic to all other devices connected to it. In effect, this cuts the Internet access of any device that used the router.

In order to launch a ping denial-of-service attack, the malicious hacker first needs to find out the IP of the victim's computer or device. This is a relatively straightforward task. Let's say you want to hack **www.testingrecipes.in**. Go to command prompt and type ping **www.testingrecipes.in**. Refer to the screen capture below:

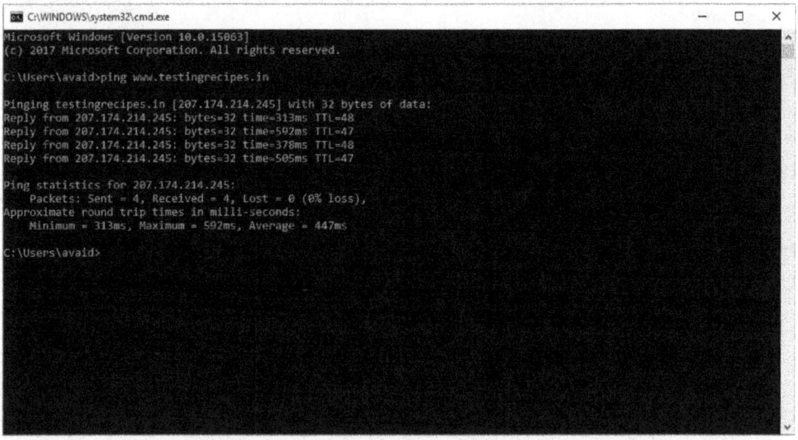

Figure 25 - Finding IP address of Target Website

From the screen capture you know that the target website's IP address is

207.174.214.245.

A ping of death is small in scale, and basic, so it's mostly efficient against small websites. However, if multiple computers come together, it's possible for a handful of these to bring down a website without the proper infrastructure to deal with this threat. Please refer to Figure 26 for the command, just replace the localhost (127.0.0.1), with the target website and try bringing it down.

Note – In order to avoid Ping of Death attacks, and its variants, many sites block ICMP ping messages at their firewalls. In case you are lucky, you will get through or else, you will need to go via DDoS

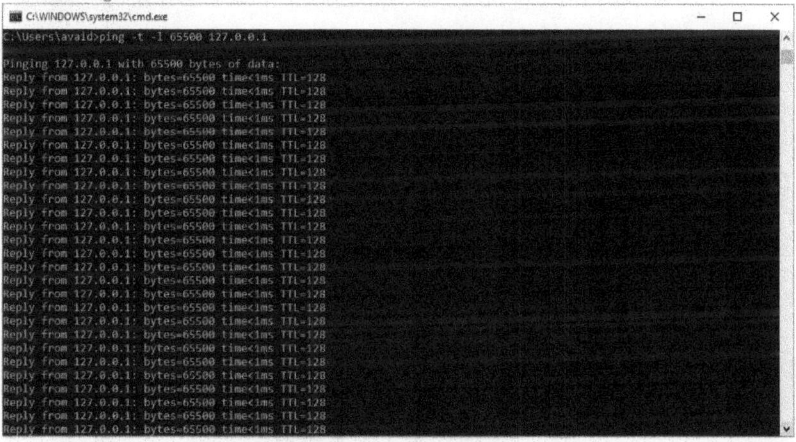

Figure 26 - Ping of Death Command

Hacking Wireless Networks

Nowadays, there are wireless hotspots everywhere! You can get internet access with a wireless enabled laptop almost everywhere you go. In this chapter we will discuss ways a hacker goes about getting into secure wireless networks and things he can do once he is inside.

Scanning for Wireless Networks

For this section and the following, you will need to have a wireless card/adapter. The hacker starts by scanning for wireless networks near him. The Windows tool we will use in this section is called NetStumbler. Also by the time you read this book, eBook MacStumbler may already be released for those of you using a Mac. Some other similar programs are:

- Kismet for Windows and Linux.
- KisMac for the Mac.

1. Download and install NetStumbler.
2. Run it.
3. It will start searching for wireless access points
4. Once it is completed, you will see a list of all the wireless access points around you. Refer to Figure 27.

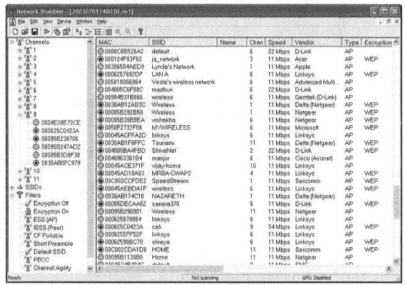

Figure 27 - Net Stumbler

5. Now click on MAC address of any of the discovered wireless networks under channels, a graph will be displayed highlighting the wireless network's signal strength. The greener and the less spaces, the better the signal. Refer to Figure 28.

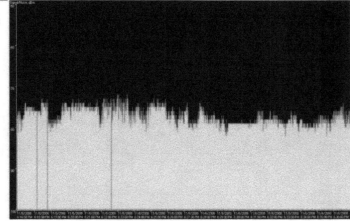

Figure 28 - Discovered Wireless Networks

6. As you can notice, NetStumbler provides a lot more than just the name (SSID) of the wireless network. It provides the MAC address, Channel number, encryption type, and so on. The entire information aids the hacker to get inside secured network by cracking the encryption.

   The most common types of encryption are:

   - WEP (Wired Equivalent Privacy) – WEP isn't considered safe anymore. Many flaws have been discovered that allow a hacker to crack a WEP key easily.

   - WAP (Wireless Application Protocol) – WAP is the currently the most secure and best option to secure any wireless network. It's not easy to crack as WEP because the only way to retrieve a WAP key is to use a brute-force or dictionary attack. If the key is secure enough, a dictionary attack won't work and it could take decades to crack it if you brute-force it. This is why most hackers don't even bother.

Cracking WEP

In this section we will use be using the Live Linux distribution called BackTrack to crack WEP. Backtrack comes with a huge list of preloaded software for this very purpose. Before we begin, there are a couple requirements:

1. You need a computer with a compatible wireless adapter.
2. Download Backtrack and create a Live CD.

The tools we will be using on Backtrack are:

- Kismet – a wireless network detector
- airodump – captures packets from a wireless router
- aireplay – forges ARP requests
- aircrack – decrypts the WEP keys

Let's start hacking –

1. First let us find a wireless access point along with its essid, bssid, and channel number. To do this we will run kismet by opening the terminal and typing in kismet. It may ask for the appropriate adapter which in this example is ath0. You can see the device's name by typing in the command iwconfig.

Figure 29 - ESSID

2. To be able to do some of the later things, the wireless adapter must be put into monitor mode. Kismet automatically does this and as long as it is open, the wireless adapter will stay in monitor mode.

3. In kismet you will see the flags Y/N/0. Each one stands for a different type of encryption. In our case we will be looking for access points with the **WEP** encryption. **Y=WEP N=OPEN 0=OTHER** (usually WAP).

4. Once you find an access point, open a text document and paste in the networks broadcast name (essid), its mac address (bssid) and its channel number. To get the above information, use the arrow keys to select an access point and hit <ENTER> to get additional information.

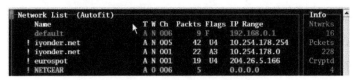

Figure 30 - Network List

5. The next step is to start collecting data from the access point with airodump. Open up a new terminal and start airodump by typing in the command:

   airodump-ng -c [channel#] -w [filename] --bssid [bssid] [device]

   In the above command airodump-ng starts the program, the channel of the access point goes after **-c**, the file you wish to output the data goes after **-w**, and the MAC address of the access point goes after **--bssid**. The command ends with the device name.

6. Leave the above program running and open another terminal.

7. A few fake packets need to be generated to the target access point so that the speed of the data output will increase. Use the following command:

aireplay-ng -1 0 -a [bssid] -h 00:11:22:33:44:55:66 -e [essid] [device]

In the above command we are using the airplay-ng program. The **-1** tells the program the specific attack we wish to use which in this case is fake authentication with the access point. The **0** cites the delay between attacks, **-a** is the MAC address of the target access point, **-h** is the wireless adapters MAC address, **-e** is the name (essid) of the target access point, and the command ends with the wireless adapter's device name.

8. Now, we will force the target access point to send out a huge number of packets that we will be able to take advantage of by using them to attempt to crack the WEP key. Once the following command is executed, check your airodump-ng terminal and you should see the ARP packet count to start to increase. The command is:

aireplay-ng -3 -b [bssid] -h 00:11:22:33:44:5:66 [device]

In this command, the **-3** tells the program the specific type of attack which in this case is packet injection, **-b** is the MAC address of the target access point, **-h** is your wireless adapters MAC address, and the wireless adapter device name goes at the end.

9. Once you have collected around 50k-500k packets, you may begin the attempt to break the WEP key. The command to begin the cracking process is:

aircrack-ng -a 1 -b [bssid] -n 128 [filename].ivs

In this command the **-a 1** forces the program into the WEP attack mode, the **-b** is the targets MAC address, and the **-n 128** tells the program the WEP key length. If you don't know the **-n** , then leave it out. This should crack the WEP key within seconds. The more packets you capture, the bigger chance you have of cracking the WEP key.

```
KB   depth   byte(vote)
 0    0/   1    7D(170496) DD(150528) 5A(148992) E8(148480) 3E(146944) 4D(146432) 82(146176)
 1    0/   1    00(172800) 52(154880) 1D(153600) 40(151040) EB(150528) F9(148480) 44(147200)
 2    0/   1    05(178176) 55(151552) 58(149760) 71(148736) 86(146944) D7(146432) 5C(145920)
 3    0/   1    F9(180736) DE(148736) 4A(147968) 52(147968) E8(147712) EF(146688) 9A(145920)
 4    0/   1    8D(173568) 80(154112) D4(148480) 4A(147968) 56(147200) 74(146176) F9(146176)
 5    0/   1    C9(176128) 62(146176) 3F(145920) 9F(145920) 87(145408) 5E(144384) A8(144384)
 6    0/   1    E4(174336) F7(151296) BE(149760) 6B(148224) F2(146432) 42(146176) 4E(145920)
 7    0/   1    89(154880) 82(153600) 5E(153088) 26(150528) 56(149760) 03(148480) 1E(147968)
 8    0/   1    F2(170240) 6A(148224) DA(147456) 62(146688) 77(146688) D8(145920) 26(144896)
 9    0/   1    11(179456) 30(153600) 9D(146688) A9(145664) 7A(145408) 05(145152) C5(145152)
10    0/   1    A7(151552) AC(149504) 6F(147968) C8(146688) E3(146432) 34(146176) BD(146176)
11    0/   1    0D(151040) 56(149504) CE(148736) CD(148480) 32(146176) 80(145664) 7E(145408)
12    0/   1    98(152576) 97(151284) 25(145800) FB(145720) 48(145232) D8(144584) C0(144184)

       KEY FOUND! [ 7D:00:05:F9:8D:C9:E4:89:F2:11:C5:49:98 ]
```

Figure 31 - Key Cracked

Packet Sniffing

Packet sniffing is the art of capturing packets going through a network. With a packet sniffer, once a hacker gains access to wireless network he can intercept private information going through a network such as: usernames, passwords, IM conversations, and e-mails etc. We will use the program Wireshark do demonstrate packet sniffing. Let's show you an example.

1. Go to the website www.wireshark.org.
2. Download and install Wireshark .
3. Invoke Wireshark.
4. Navigate to the list of available capture interfaces as shown in Figure 32.

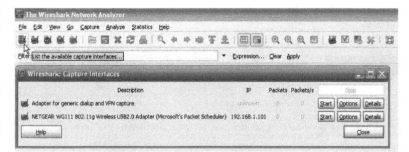

Figure 32 - Wireshark Network Adapter

Choose the target to begin capturing the packets

5. Click start

6. If you don't know which one to choose, wait for some time. The one that accumulates the most packets is always the best choice. Many captured packets validate that the targeted user is currently active.

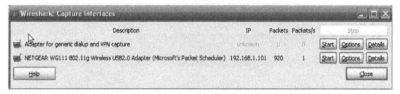

Figure 33 - Wireshark Capture Interfaces

7. As an example of how Wireshark can be used, start Windows Live and send a couple of messages. You will notice that the entire conversation is being captured/monitored. Refer to the screen capture below. In order to discard junk data, type "msnms" in the filter field.

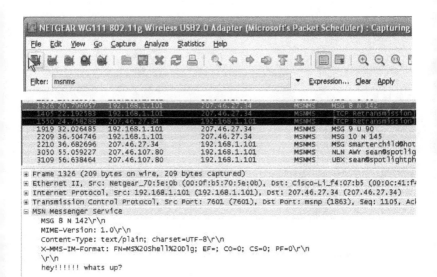

Figure 34 - Network Capturing

Notice that the junk data is gone and the message sent is being displayed in the bottom of the screen. If I continue down the list I can see the whole conversation.

Note - Usernames and passwords are captured the same way

Some other useful sniffing programs include:

- Snort
- WinDump
- Dsniff

Preventing your network from being hacked

Here are a few recommendations to stay safe while using WiFi networks:

1. Use a long secure password for your router. Include a combination of numbers, lowercase letters, uppercase letters, and special characters.

2. Ensure that the router is not broadcasting SSID, disable it in case it is. This will prevent programs like Net Stumbler from locating your wireless network.

3. Use MAC filtering on your router. Every wireless card and wireless adapter has a MAC address. By choosing to allow only your MAC addresses onto the network, you can keep a lot of attackers out.

4. To prevent packet sniffing attacks from affecting you, make sure the important sites you use, like banks, use SSL (Secure Socket Layer) encryption. You can tell if the site has SSL enabled if the URL begins with "https" instead of "http".

5. Change the default password of router and ensure that WAP encryption is enabled. If the router doesn't have a WAP option, use WEP.

6. In internet cafes or other hotspots where internet is free, packet sniffing is very common. To avoid being affected use a VPN (Virtual Private Network) service to encrypt the data you send across the internet.

Using Malware to hack

Malware is one of the biggest nuisances in the world of Cyber Crime. The most common types of malware happen to be viruses, worms, and trojan horses. Before diving into details, let's get familiar with vocabulary.

1. **What is a Virus** – A virus is a self-propagating program once triggered. The first virus was created by a Pakistani on a DOS

platform and was spread through floppy disks. But now in the world of intranet and internet, viruses thrive. I have myself never created a virus but have done some live virus testing. For testing the effectiveness of anti-virus, the best way is to use the test viruses (eicar and tryguard). Viruses are like parasites because they need a host to attach themselves to. The host is typically a legitimate looking program or file. Once this program is launched, the virus is executed and infects other files on the target computer. Viruses can be very destructive. They can do damage to your computer hardware, software and files. Viruses are spread through the sharing of files and are many times sent within emails via attachments. They are sometimes termed by catchy names to entice the target. For example, there was a virus by the name of iloveyou.vbs, which spread like wildfire.

2. **What is a Trojan Horse – Trojan horse**, or **trojan**, is any malware which misleads users of its true intent. The term is derived from the Ancient Greek story of the deceptive Trojan Horse that led to the fall of the city of Troy.

   Trojans are generally spread by some form of social engineering, for example where a user is duped into executing an email attachment disguised to appear not suspicious, (e.g., a routine form to be filled in), or by clicking on some fake advertisement on social media or anywhere else. Although their payload can be anything, many modern forms act as a backdoor, contacting a controller which can then have unauthorized access to the affected computer. Trojans may allow an attacker to access users' personal information such as banking information, passwords, or personal identity. It can also delete a user's files or infect other devices connected to the network. Ransomware attacks are often carried out using a trojan.

3. **What is a Worm** – A worm is a malicious program that can replicate itself onto other computers on a network. Unlike a virus, worms don't need a human to be able to spread and infect systems. Once it infects a system, it uses that system to send out other copies of itself to other random systems attempting to infect them.

4. **What are Logic Bombs** – Logic bombs are usually pieces of code that are programmed into a program that lie dormant until a certain time or until a user does a certain action which causes it to be executed. When it is triggered it performs a certain function that the program wasn't intended to do.

5. **What are Blended Threats** – Blended threats combine all of the characteristics of the above and use them along with system vulnerabilities to spread and infect machines.

Using ProRat for Hacking

In order to download ProRat. Go to the following site -
https://prorat.software.informer.com/1.9/
While extracting the zip file, it will prompt with a password (refer to Figure below). The password is pro

Figure 35 Enter Password for ProRat

Double click ProRat.exe as displayed in the figure below:

ProRat configuration screen will be displayed as shown in Figure 32

Figure 36 - ProRat Configuration Screen

On the left bottom of the screen, Click button. Following screen will be displayed:

Figure 37 - Using Create to Invoke ProRat Server

Click Create ProRat Server

Create Server screen will be displayed as shown in Figure 34

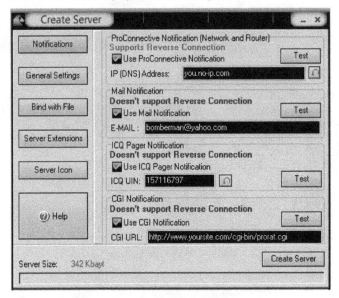

Figure 38 - Create ProRat Server

Enter your IP Address in the first field. You can use IPConfig command in Command prompt to find your IP address. Alternatively, click the arrow next to the field. It will auto populate your IP address. Add your email address. This is the get a notification whenever a victim gets infected.

Click on General Settings. Following screen will be displayed. You can choose the port, password to enter when victim gets infected and the victim name. You can leave the settings as is or change them based on your preferences.

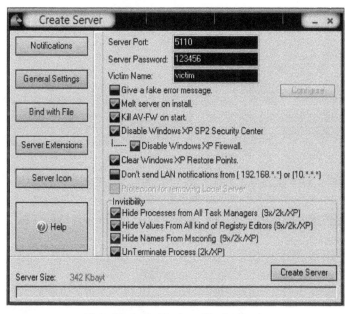

Figure 39 - General Settings of ProRat Server

Click on Bind with File. Following screen will be displayed. Click Bind server with a file check box. This will enable the Select File button. Click on Select File button.

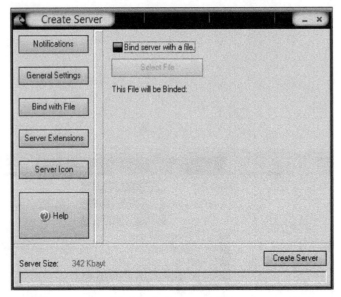

Figure 40 - Bind Server with a file

Note – it is important to bind the Trojan Server to a file because it will only execute it if the end user executes it. For the purpose of demonstration, I am binding it to my picture. Use your creativity here and bind the server to a file which the end user is most likely to click.

Figure 41 - Binding Server to Image File

Click on confirmation dialog box as shown in Figure 38 below:

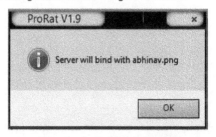

Figure 42 - Confirmation Dialog Box

Click on Server Extensions button. Following dialog box will be displayed. Select either exe or SCR since it has icon support to change. Certainly change the icon in case you are selecting the default exe, which will look suspicious to end user.

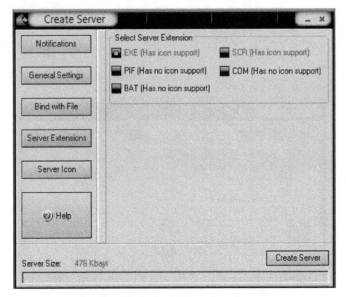

Figure 43 - Configuring Server Extensions

Click on the Server Icon Button. Following dialog box will be displayed. This helps in masking the actual server file. I am selecting an image since I have used my image.

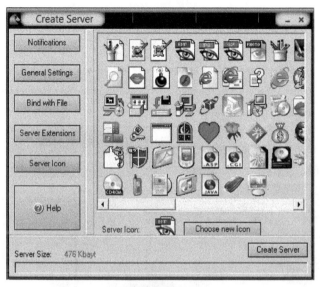

Figure 44 - Create Server

Click Create Server. The server will be created and you will receive a confirmation dialog box as shown in Figure below:

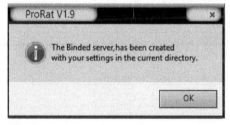

Go to the directory where the binded server file is placed. In this case, it looks like the one displayed in Figure below

Now rename it to something like Iloveyou or something and send it to intended recipient. You could also post it to some media site as a movie available for download. Let's say the user has clicked it and Trojan has activated/installed at the end users

machine. Note that it will run in the background and the end user will never know about it.

The moment end user has done it, I or the intended hacker will receive an email prompt confirming the end user has been infected.

Now Run the Server on your machine and give the IP address and, port number and hit the connect button. . You will be prompted for a password, enter the password and hit enter. Refer to screen capture below:

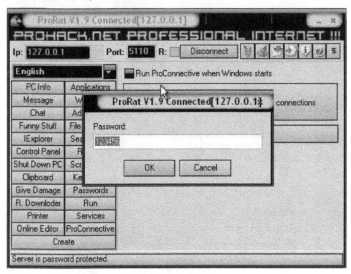

Figure 45 - Configuring Password

Bingo, you have control over the target computer.

Now you can play with a lot of options as displayed in Figure 42. You can hide desktop options, hide start button and so on. You have full rights to all the files on the target computer. Let's do some fun on the target computer

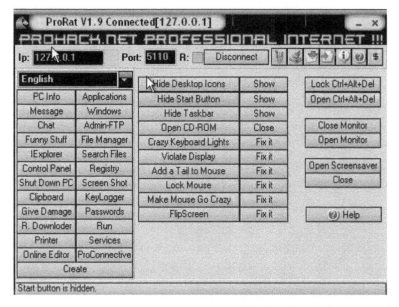

Figure 46 - Playing with Infected Computer

Send a message to the target computer that he has been hacked.

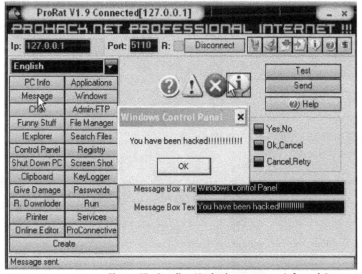

Figure 47 - Sending Hacked message to Infected Computer

Note – I will not go into more details as you can unleash your
creativity here

Introduction to Cyber Crime and Espionage

Cyber crime and espionage have become the reality of our world. There have been some efforts by various Governments but a step wise methodical approach to curb these challenges must evolve. One must recognize first that the enemy lies within before one begins to master those who threaten from external points. Knowledge must evolve and develop a sense of vigilance that lends itself to the development and proliferation of those who seek to combat the actions of the criminally inclined. It encourages and enables to detect, identify, and prevent criminal activity and gain a greater degree of insight into the psychological motivations and drivers at work within these individuals and groups while enabling a more robust understanding of the tactics, strategies, and plans being executed on a global basis to accomplish their means. A new breed of information security professionals must be armed and equipped with the tools necessary for addressing these adversaries and their actions.

Espionage or **spying** is the act of obtaining secret or confidential information or without legal permission of the holder of information. Any individual or spy ring (a cooperating group of spies), in the service of a government, company or independent operation, can commit espionage. In some circumstances it may be a legal tool of law enforcement and in others it may be illegal and punishable by law. Espionage is a method of gathering which includes information gathering from non-disclosed sources.

Espionage is often a part of an institutional effort by a government or commercial concern. However, the term tends to be associated with state spying on potential or actual enemies for military purposes. Spying involving corporations is known as industrial espionage.

One of the most effective ways to gather data and information about a targeted organization is by infiltrating its ranks. This is the job of the spy (espionage agent). Spies can then return information such as the size and strength of enemy forces. They can also find dissidents within the organization and influence them to provide further information or to defect. In times of crisis, spies steal technology and sabotage the enemy in various ways. Counterintelligence is the practice of thwarting enemy espionage and intelligence-gathering. Almost all nations have strict laws concerning espionage and the penalty for being caught is often severe. However, the benefits obtained through espionage are far greater that prompts governments and organizations to go ahead and use it.

Lately, the global village as we call it has exposed us to transparent and technological world, the ability to control private information on internet or the one exposed via our mobile has exposed us to unlimited exposure. This is not limited to email retrieval by third parties, social media like Facebook, data mining, search engine, GPS etc.

Vulnerable Technologies –

Mobile devices have become an indispensable asset that everyone uses extensively. The smartphones track what you do, where you go, what you search on the internet to pretty much everything and the data is commercialized to send you targeted ads etc. and, in a way, invades your privacy.

The social media has exposed us to an array of privacy and security issues. The large amounts of information stored in Facebook, Instagram, MySpace, and Google etc. can be used to portray a complete personal profile of anyone who uses these services. Using an Android phone, you will need to configure gmail to make it to work and by default everywhere you go right from restaurants, pubs, malls etc. will be tracked and stored on google servers. Anyone who can get into your gmail can track your entire activity.

Government Abuse of Cybersecurity and Espionage

In the year 2013, Edward Snowden exposed thousands of classified documents that revealed global surveillance program in association with several other countries. The program was called "Five Eyes". ECHELON was another secret government surveillance program (signals intelligence/SIGINT collection and analysis network) operated by the United States with the aid of four other signatory states to the UKUSA Security Agreement: Australia, Canada, New Zealand, and the United

Kingdom, also known as the Five Eyes.

Former NSA analyst Perry Fellwock, under pseudonym Winslow Peck, first blew the whistle on ECHELON to Ramparts, where he gave commentary revealing a global network of listening posts and his experiences working there. Fellwock also included revelations such as the existence of nuclear weapons in Israel in 1972, the widespread involvement of CIA and NSA personnel in drugs and human smuggling, and CIA operatives leading Nationalist Chinese (Taiwan) commandos in burning villages inside PRC borders.

The Government bodies are also known to do espionage either on their own or with the help of private players. Public incidents also happen including both Government and Military. There is a counter cybercrime Organization that works with various security companies and does international digital investigations and also co-ordinate with various countries since the crime is global. A very popular intrusion on the computer network of Norwegian telecommunications company Telenor was the result of a large cyberespionage operation of Indian origin that for many and had targeted business, government and political organizations from different countries, according to researchers from security firm Norman Shark.

Researchers from Norman analyzed the malware samples used in the attack on Telenor, which started out with spear-phishing emails sent to the company's senior management, after receiving information about them from the Norwegian Computer Emergency Response Team (NorCERT).

During their investigation, the Norman researchers established correlations between that attack's command-and-control infrastructure and other malware and domain names, discovering what appeared to be an ongoing large-scale cyberespionage operation of Indian origin that was active for almost three years.

The operation was dubbed HangOver and started somewhere around September 2010 and was discovered in 2013. The attackers targeted business, government and political organizations, including targets of national security interest from Pakistan, separatist groups from India and companies from different industries from the U.S. and other countries.

The main attack method seemed to be spear-phishing emails, which incorporate malicious attachments and are crafted according to the interests of each target. Although no proofs were shared to blame India for the attack, although a company Appin Security Group (a New Delhi based company from India) was named as creator of attack.

Chapter - Other Traits and Best Practices

Staying Safe – Importance and Measures

No activity you do on the Internet is safe and every click done on the Internet has a potential to be tracked to source. This should not be an issue, as long as the intentions are right. Still, there are a few tools recommended.

Kali Linux –

1. Kali Linux is a Linux distribution and by far the most popular Operating System of choice of hacking community. It comes pre bundled with tools that are handy to perform various hacking activities. It makes it easier for the hacker, which otherwise becomes a harder task as one needs to install add-ons or tools to perform tasks.

2. A few steps, tools/techniques mentioned in the current book makes the system vulnerable to security. This is required because one to disable the anti virus and other scanners, which block the access to the tools. On the other hand, having a Kali distribution comes in handy because one can directly boot using Kali and thus

prevent the system for any potential security risks.

3. To understand the possibilities without extra effort, please refer to the Figure 48

Figure 48 - Supported Tools Kali Linux

Ref – www.kalilinux.org

Tip – In contrary to what many believe, Kali Linux is not hard to learn. In fact, the user-friendly GUI driven Interface makes it a breeze. Moreover, one does not even need to install it. You can just burn it to a CD and run boot it via Kali.

World of Browsers -

Tor browser –

Tor is the safest browser to cover the tracks and stay anonymous on the Internet. In order to download, go to www.tor.com. It can be used to go to .onion sites (sites on hidden web). It displays an interface as shown in Figure 45.

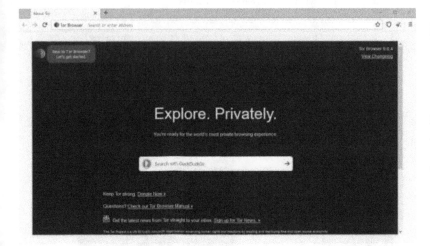

Figure 49 - Tor Browser

I2P –

I2P is by all means the safest and the most secure browser. It is extremely configurable and supported by a user-friendly interface and developers.

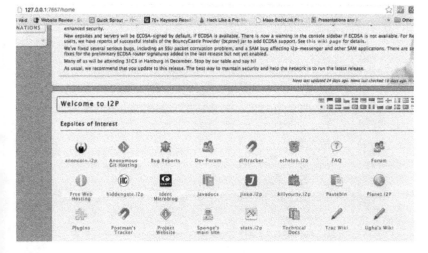

Figure 50 - Interface I2P Browser

Using Firefox Plugins -

Firefox browser comes with some plugins that can be downloaded as ad-ons to perform various tasks. Some of the popular plugins include

Live Headers –

Live headers is an awesome plugin used to automate/play with the network traffic. In order to use it, perform the following steps:

1. Install the Live Headers plugin on Firefox Browser

2. Go to the favorite site (in this case it is Testing Recipes)

3. Invoke the Live Headers.

4. In case there are any logs etc., clear them and then Click the **capture**

check box as shown in Figure 47

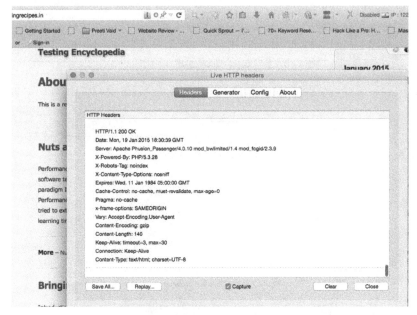

Figure 51 - Live Headers

This can be saved or replayed. The Replay option will keep repeating the action performed previously and keep increasing the count that hits the server. Now imagine going to Facebook page and finding out the like control and then playing with it.

Tamper data –

Tamper data plug in used to play and tamper the network traffic. In order to use it, perform the following steps:

1. Invoke Firefox

2. Install the Tamper data add-on

3. Invoke the Add-on (displayed in Figure 48) and see the possibilities.

Note - Careful while you play with tamper data because in case you do not own the website/application, doing something, which you do not understand, could be fatal.

For example, there was a bug in Hotmail.com, where playing with numbers could result in bye-passing the servers and making an entry. Tamper data could be the ideal tool for that.

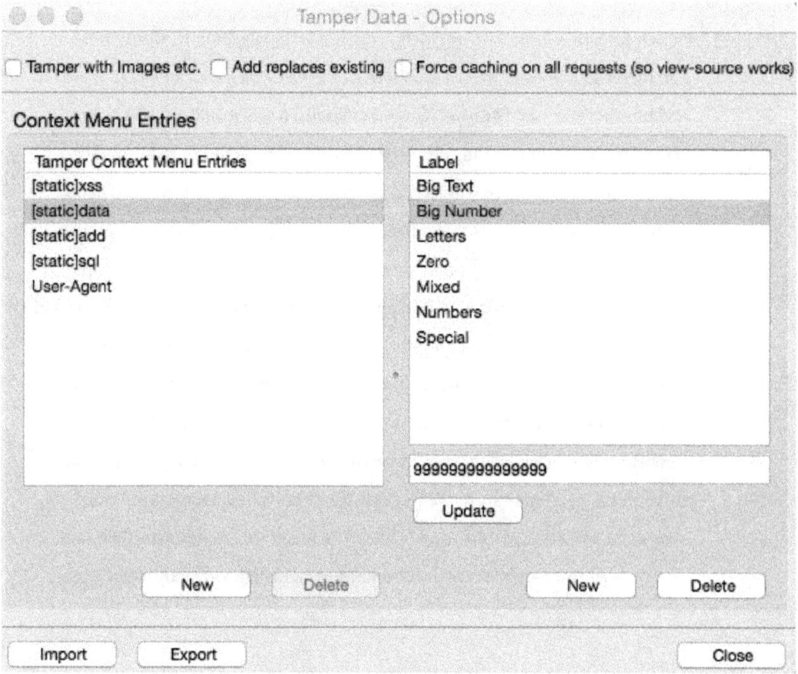

Figure 52 - Tamper data using Firefox

Other Tricks and Possibilities –

All the below mentioned tricks have been fairly tested and doable, try doing research and achieving the targets. Come back to publisher in case you need help.

1. Creating 1000 Hotmail accounts – in one click
2. Scaling up real world network Traffic gracefully – using 3 steps
3. Sending mail from Bill Gates billg@microsoft.com
4. Getting 10000 facebook likes

Don't go there –

1. **4Chan culture** – 4Chan(https://4chan.org/) was initially built by Chris Poole. He had taken source code from a Japanese site 2chan which was an imageboard and tailored it to build 4Chan. To me it looks like a sadist culture. Lulz is an acronym used to define the culture of 4Chan i.e., taking pleasure in someone else's misery. It's a board where you can post any pictures anonymously and then add content to it. If it is liked/replied to, it stays, otherwise it goes down quickly. Their creative and innovative techniques have done a lot of disruption over the web. It is very easy to find people with similar disruptive intentions and then use it against intended targets. They also post DDoS techniques over the site and invite members to attack the intended targets. One of the biggest attack they did was in support of Julian Assange (founder of WikiLeaks). They launched Operation Payback in support of Julian Assange when a few payment companies stopped taking donations for WikiLeaks. 4Chan launched coordinated DDoS attacks on MasterCard, Visa, and PayPal. The result was that MasterCard and Visa sites were brought down and PayPal was slowed down resulting in huge

latencies. A lot of anonymous group members are very active in 4Chan.

2. **Anonymous** – We are Anonymous, We will be Back

This group had received a lot of attention due to Sony incident. Well, the exact motivation and the source of Anonymous Team member/s was involved is still unknown. And what intentions (The Interview – movie) was just one of the files from huge data that was pulled out. This becomes an illegal intent because it has resulted in a financial dent on the Organization. Not to forget about hundreds of cascading effects of this incident including threatening mails claiming to bomb Theatres and sharing the personal data of employees. Unless you are serious about hacking and understand nuts and bolts of hacking, do not get associated with Anonymous group.

This group was never supposed to go Political. Although, there was no face or a representative, but then there were people from all around the world standing up for the right cause. They still have their own forums, IRC Channels, meetings and so on where they communicate with others using their pen names. This group, at least initially stood up for the right cause and brought out the facts, which were otherwise either ignored or stopped due to Political reasons. A few incidents of commendable works by them include –

1. Bringing out the rape case of a minor by a team of Football Players

2. Bringing out War Crimes, that had been oppressed by Law Enforcing Agencies or kept as secrets

3. Bringing out black money that some Indian Politicians had stored in Swiss Banks

One of the leading anthropologists coming from the Trolling era, who has been very closely communicating with them released a book – "hackers, crackers, whistle blowers…". She still feels that Anonymous is a great concept and the class and intentions of people associated are commendable.

4. The Lizards –

This is another community that claims to be benchmarking with the Anonymous but be very careful. There is absolutely no evidence whatsoever to prove that the group is a legitimate or a crime.

5. The Deep Web –

The Deep Web is a name given to a separate network, which remains invisible to the general public on the World Wide Web. The sites are not indexed by the usual search engine and are known as Onion Sites. The name was possibly chosen due to design that has gone into building the Architecture (beyond the scope of the current book). Although, refer to the screen capture displayed in Figure 49 to have a cursory glimpse of what it is –

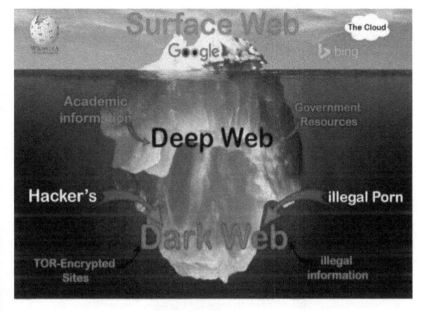

Figure 53 - Deep Web

The opposite term to the deep web is the "surface web", which is accessible to anyone/everyone using the Internet. Computer-scientist Michael K. Bergman is credited with coining the term deep web in 2001 as a search-indexing term.

The content of the deep web can be located and accessed by a direct URL or IP address, but may require a password or other security access to get past public-website pages. The dark web is also a part of deep web.

What is Dark Web

The dark web is a part of deep web and therefore not indexed by search engines. The dark web is popular mostly for criminal activities. As per a study in 2015, from 2,723 live dark web sites revealed that 57% host illicit material.

Another study in 2019 study, Into the Web of Profit, conducted by Dr. Michael McGuires at the University of Surrey, shows that things have become worse. The number of dark web listings that could harm an enterprise has risen by 20% since 2016. Of all listings (excluding those selling drugs), 60% could potentially harm enterprises.

Anyone can buy drugs, credit card numbers, guns, counterfeit money, stolen subscription credentials, hacked Netflix accounts and software that helps you break into other people's computers. You can also buy usernames and passwords.

However, as mentioned earlier, not everything is illegal in darknet for example, you can join a chess club, a social network often called as "the Facebook of Tor network."

Deep web vs. dark web

The terms "deep web" and "dark web" are often used interchangeably, but they are not the same. Deep web refers to anything on the internet that is not indexed by and, therefore, accessible via a search engine like Google. Deep web content includes anything behind a paywall or requires sign-in credentials. It also includes any content that its owners have blocked web crawlers from indexing. The websites use roborts.txt file to exclude the files/folders that do not need to be indexed by search engines.

Medical records, fee-based content, membership websites, and confidential corporate web pages are just a few examples of what makes up the deep web. Estimates place the size of the deep web at between 96% and 99% of the internet. Only a tiny portion of the internet is accessible through a standard web browser often called as surface web.

The dark web is a subset of the deep web that is intentionally hidden, requiring a specific browser for example Tor to access. No one really knows the size of the dark web, but most estimates put it at around 5% of the total internet. Again, not all the dark web is used for illicit purposes despite its ominous-sounding name.

Risks due to dark web tools and technologies

Following tools, technologies and techniques present key risk -

1. Phishing
2. Refunds
3. Customer data
4. Operational data
5. Financial data
6. Intellectual property/trade secrets
7. Other emerging threats
8. Infection or attacks, including malware, botnets etc.
9. Access, including remote access Trojans (RATs), keyloggers and exploits
10. Espionage, including services, customization and targeting
11. Support services such as tutorials
12. End user Credentials

Dark web browser

It is not easy to browse through dark web. Tor browser, discussed later is used to access deep web or dark web.

Dark web search engine

Two search engines are popular in Dark web i.e., the Hidden Wiki and Grams.

Dark web sites

The dark web sites use .onion as an extension instead of .com/.us etc. Tor browser with the help of proxy servers aid in reaching these web sites.

Dark web sites also use a twisted naming structure that creates URLs that are often difficult to remember. For example, a popular commerce site called Dream Market goes by the unintelligible address of "088enu9343159814ab.onion."

The dark websites are typically created by geeks with criminal intentions, who keep move around to avoid the wrath of their victims. Even commercial sites that may have existed for a while can suddenly disappear.

Financial transactions on Dark web

The financial transactions have thrived in dark web due to bitcoin. Bitcoin is a crypto-currency that enables two parties to conduct a trusted transaction without knowing each other's identity. According to Tiquet, "Bitcoin has been a major factor in the growth of the dark web, and the dark web has been a big factor in the growth of bitcoin,"

Nearly all dark web commerce sites conduct transactions in bitcoin or similar currency, but that doesn't mean it's safe to do business. The inherent anonymity of the place attracts scammers and thieves, but what do you expect when buying guns or drugs is your objective?

Dark web commerce sites have the same features as any e-retail operation, including ratings/reviews, shopping carts and forums, but there are important differences. One is quality control. When both buyers and sellers are anonymous, the credibility of any ratings system is dubious. Ratings are easily manipulated, and even sellers with long track records have been known to suddenly disappear with their customers' crypto-coins, only to set up shop later under a different alias. Also, some governing bodies are closely monitoring the ecommerce activities in dark web. The silk road was one example that was cracked by Government. **Silk Road** was an online black market and the first modern darknet market, best known as a platform for selling illegal drugs. As part of the dark web, it was operated as a Tor hidden service, such that online users were able to browse it anonymously and securely without potential traffic monitoring. The website was launched in February 2011; development had begun six months prior. Initially there were a limited number of new seller accounts available; new sellers had to purchase an account in an auction. Later, a fixed fee was charged for each new seller account.

Most e-commerce providers offer some kind of service that keeps customer funds on hold until the product has been delivered. However, in the event of a dispute don't expect service with a smile. It's pretty much up to the buyer and the seller to duke it out. Every communication is encrypted, so even the simplest transaction requires a PGP key.

Even completing a transaction is no guarantee that the goods will arrive. Many need to cross international borders, and customs officials are cracking down on suspicious packages. The dark web news site Deep.Dot.Web teems with stories of buyers who have been arrested or jailed for attempted purchases.

The Good Part –

In India you can report a Cyber Crime here -
https://cybercrime.gov.in/Webform/FAQ.aspx

The Evil Part –
Unfortunately, this part is scary because the FBI and other legal authorities are coming heavily on them due to the following reasons –

- ✓ It was being abused by drug dealers as well as users, as it turned out to be the safest option. The Silk Road was the most notorious among them
- ✓ It was being used to hire Hitmen and the people seeking their services. With both parties being anonymous, it becomes almost impossible for the Government agencies to trace.
- ✓ Terrorists from various parts of the world started using it and it is quiet common to see Weapons of Mass destruction being traded
5. Currency – The crypto/digital currency being used is called **bitcoin**. Since this is

not under normal currencies, it makes it virtually impossible for Governments to track.

Note – Make your Informed Choice and do not get trapped.

Chapter - The Road Ahead

This is just a start, keep the book handy as an archive for reference. Pick a hacking topic of choice and move higher on the hacking skills. A few valuable resources -

1. <u>Astalavista</u> – it one point of time, it used to be the most popular hacking site. Although the popularity has decreased, it is still regarded as a key source for hacking tools and papers.

2. <u>HackThisSite</u> – this is my all-time favorite site. It includes real world examples which one can try and learn during the process and the hacker would know how he is scaling his skill sets as compared to others.

3. <u>HellBound Hackers</u> - Another popular hacking website.

4. <u>Black-Hat Forums</u> – a very popular and engaging hacking forum

5. <u>https://www.hellboundhackers.org/</u> - a great site about learning about exploits along with a lot of hacking challenges including website hacking, app hacking.

Security Communities –

OWASP is one of the most reputed Organization leading initiatives in all aspects of hacking and network security. Ref – www.owasp.org

Chapter - Why are we here?

This is indeed a very difficult question, but the most fundamental and gruesome reasons are –

Ethics and Law Enforcement

Fate of Whistle Blowers –

Since the time in memorial, except for a few and rare cases, whistle blowers have always been crushed. NASA spaceship disaster could have very well be presented. The Organization learnt it at the cost of lives of people, but that was not the end. The careers of whistleblowers were jeopardy.

The latest cases are Wikileaks and the after-effects on Bradley Manning and Julian's stories are available all around the globe.

Organizational Issues –

To stay ahead in completion, the Organizations release the products that are not market ready.

7 Layers of Network –

While releasing the Products, Organizations often ignore the importance of what would happen when the product/service hits the market. For example, there are vulnerabilities specific to the network layers, which are rarely tested.

Testing is performed as a bye product rather than integrated with the Software Development Life Cycle. So even if the Security Test Team finds out a nasty bug, the engineering Team will probably defer it or mark it as a low Priority. And it does make business sense to do it that way, but then what's the point of doing the Testing, maybe either a formality or an informed risk so that there are no surprises when the product goes live. Refer to Figure 26, which displays how Security Testing is integrated into the lifecycle (this is the general trend followed by most of the companies).

What can be done for a safer environment?

Security Testing should be integrated as a part of software lifecycle, and there should be measure able/quantified metrics. This in turn, to a very large extent help Organizations to fix defects during early phases (less expensive) and then it will also give an objective indicator of what's the risk on Society, People, Product, and the Organization. A small spreadsheet (Figure displayed below) can make a significant impact and help everyone to make more informed choices.

35 Steps to a Safer Web Experience

At the first place, Security Considerations should be considered at the Requirements Phase itself. Even if it is not, having a small metric with just 35 Tests can make the biggest difference.

Is this so hard?

S.No	Category	Test Name	Test Scope	Tests Steps
1		Spiders, Robots and Crawlers		Analyze Robots.txt using Webmaster Tools
2		Search Engine Discovery/Reconnaissance	Information obtained with help of Search Engines	Search google with various google dorks
3		Identify application entry points		Identify form parameters, methods HTTP Header analysis
4	Information Gathering	Testing for Web Application Fingerprint	WebServer Details Enumeration	Analyse the HTTP headers
5		Application Discovery	find Applications hosted in the webserver, non standard ports,	Google for subdomain discovery, Network Tools
6		Analysis of Error Codes	Grab information disclosed in error codes	Request random page, Login Failed, Remove/add request parameters,Denied dir listing, Create network issues
7	Configuration Management Testing	SSL/TLS Testing (SSL Version, Algorithms, Key length, Digital Cert. Validity) - SSL Weakness		Identify SSL service, ciphers, analyse certificate expiry

8		Infrastructure Configuration Management Testing - Infrastructure Configuration management weakness	Config management for webserver software, back-end database servers, auth servers.	Understand the infrastructure elements interactions, Admin tools review, Ports used, Version check.
9		Old, backup and unreferenced files - Old, backup and unreferenced files	Accessing and downloading the backup files which can escape the file restrictions	Check for On-the-fly backup files created, Check comments, Check JS source code, Random guessing of filename, Directory Listing, Search cached files
10		Infrastructure and Application Admin Interfaces - Access to Admin interfaces	Try to exploit the admin functions such as User Allocation, Site design/layout, Data manipulation, Configs	Directory and file enumeration, Comments and links in source, Reviewing server and application docs, Alternative server port, Parameter tampering, Seperation of duties check
11		Testing for HTTP Methods and XST - HTTP Methods enabled, XST permitted, HTTP Verb		Disable PUT, DELETE, CONNECT, TRACE can be checked by using OPTIONS command, XST Testing- Inject JS with Trace comman, XSRF Test-check for HEAD /request

12		Credentials transport over an encrypted channel - Credentials transport over an encrypted channel		Check referrer whether its HTTP or HTTPS, Check the method used
13	Authentication Testing	Brute Force Testing - Credentials Brute forcing		Dictionary, Search, Rule-Based (pswd masks) Bruteforce attacks
14		Testing for bypassing authentication schema - Bypassing authentication schema		Forward Browsing, Param Modification,Session ID Predication (Session Hijacking), SQL Injection
15	Session Management	Testing for Session Management Schema - Bypassing Session Management Schema, Weak Session Token	CookieCollection,CookieReverseEngineering,CookieManipulation.	Unencrypted Cookie Transport,Presence of persistent cookies,Cache-Control Settings, SessionID Analysis-SensitiveInfo, Randomness, Cryptanalysis, BruteForce
16		Testing for Cookies attributes - Cookies are set not 'HTTP Only', 'Secure', and no time validity		";secure", HTTPOnly - Always set, "; domain=app.mysite.com", "; path=/myapp/", expires-Future Value => inspect for sensitive data

17		Testing for Session Fixation - Session Fixation	The application doesn't renew the cookie after auth -Session hijacking	
18		Testing for Exposed Session Variables - Exposed sensitive session variables		Encryption & Reuse of Session To kens vulnerabilities, Proxies & Caching vulnerabilities, TGET & POST vulnerabilities, Tra nsport vulnerabilities
19	Authorizati on Testing	Testing for Path Traversal - Path Traversal	Proper Implementation of ACLs, Check server side includes	a) Input vector enumeration b) Testing Techniques dot-dot-slash attack (../), directory traversal,directory climbing, or backtracking
20		Testing for bypassing authorization schema - Bypassing authorization schema		Access a resource without authentication/after logout, Forceful Browsing
21	Business logic testing	Testing for Business Logic - Bypassable business logic	Bypass the actual workflow required to complete a process	*Understanding the application *Creating raw data for designing logical tests (Workflows, ACLs) *Designing the logical tests *Standard prerequisites *Execution of logical tests

22		Testing for Reflected Cross Site Scripting - Reflected XSS	Check for input validation, try out different combinations of XSS vectors	1. Detect input vectors. 2. Analyze each input vector to d etect potential vulnerabilities 3. Replace the vector used to identify XSS with the vector which can exploit the vulnerability.
23		Testing for DOM based Cross Site Scripting - DOM XSS	This happens mostly due to poor javascript coding.	Test for the user inputs obtained from client-side JavaScript objects
24	Data Validation Testing	SQL Injection - SQL Injection	1.Inband (retrieved data in the webpage) 2.Out-of-band (data sent through email or other means) 3.Inferential (Analyse the behaviour of Dbserver)	**Test Categories** 1.Authentication Forms, 2.Search Engine, 3.E-Commerce sites **Tests** 1.Heuristic Analysis(' , : , --) 2.Construct SQL Injection Vectors 3.Analyse Error Messages
25		LDAP Injection - LDAP Injection		Ability to • Access unauthorized content • Evade Application restrictions • Gather unauthorized information • Add or modify Objects inside LDAP tree structure.

26		XML Injection - XML Injection		Check with XML Meta Characters ', " , <>, <!--/-->, &, <![CDATA[/]]>,
27		SSI Injection - SSI Injection		* Presense of .shtml extension * Check for these characters < ! # = / . " - > and [a-zA-Z0-9] * include String = <!--#include virtual="/etc/passwd" -->
28		XPath Injection - XPath Injection	Unlike SQL, there are not ACLs enforced, as our query can access every part of the XML document	* Check for XML error enumeration by supplying a single quote (') * Username: ' or '1' = '1 Password: ' or '1' = '1
29		IMAP/SMTP Injection - IMAP/SMTP Injection		• Exploitation of vulnerabilities in the IMAP/SMTP protocol • Application restrictions evasion • Anti-automation process evasion • Information leaks • Relay/SPAM The standard attack patterns are: • Identifying vulnerable parameters • Understanding the data flow and deployment structure of the client

				• IMAP/SMTP command injection
30		Code Injection - Code Injection		Enter commands in the input field
31		OS Commanding - OS Commanding		Understand the application platform, OS, folder structure, relative path and execute those
32		Buffer overflow - Buffer overflow	• Testing for heap overflow vulnerability • Testing for stack overflow vulnerability • Testing for format string vulnerability	
33		Incubated vulnerability - Incubated vulnerability		File Upload, Stored XSS , SQL/XPATH Injection, Manage server files via server misconfigs

34		Locking Customer Accounts - Locking Customer Accounts		Wrong Attempts Valid Username enumeration - Login Page, New User Reg Page, Password Reset Page
35		User Input as a Loop Counter - User Input as a Loop Counter		if the user can directly or indirectly assign a value that will be used as a counter in a loop function, this can cause performance problems on the server.

Figure 54 - 35 Tests to a Safer Web Experience

The Hackers –

Famous Communities and Gurus – Elite Class to follow

Anonymous – the group was never intended to become political and was purely for bringing out information, which would otherwise remain hidden or ignored. This is still a great place provided your intentions are right.

Julian Asssange– He is, to the best of our knowledge the most genuine and a person, who will not move, regardless of the consequences.

Indian Anonymous – an ex-colleague, who manages various security events, speaks in conferences, publishes books and capable of tweaking, creating, modifying viruses to spam bots. He works for an anti-virus company and can't reveal his real identity. Interested! Send me a mail and I will connect you to him.

Infamous/Self Promoted Fakes – don't get trapped

Ankit Fadia – the self-proclaimed liar, who has published more than 20 books with not even one implementation. He has also been giving Certification exams. Stay away from him.

Marketers with False Promises – verify the identities and do all kinds of referral checks.

Index

Where can we look for additional Information?

Google is your best friend. Some references are given in the related section

 Platform Coverage and Scope –

The book has been created using MAC. The work has been verified in all the popular browsers including Firefox, Chrome, and Internet Explorer. The Operating Systems used for the work include Windows 7,8,10, MAC and Kali Linux.

For readability and flow, the digital testing of supported ebook formats has been tested on multiple mobile emulators as well as on Micromax Canvas Doodle 2 (ARM/Android 4.2)

Play Safe – A Warning

There is one problem in the world of web, the process is almost irreversible. Feel free to skip this chapter, in case not interested. Sharing some experiences that only highlight how ugly things can become, in case one is not careful –

1. H.263 – It is a high-quality video format used in mobile phones. It was an innovation, destined to change how the videos were captured, transmitted, and viewed. It got released after getting integrated with the latest mobile phone by world's number one cellphone company. One of the video taken in that format by a student went viral. Result, the Managing Director of largest online store got arrested.

2. YouTube – There is a video available on YouTube by my name. It shows a birthday party being celebrated with alcohol. I am nowhere to be seen in the video, but I see a few people who look familiar and happen to be from my industry. They are drinking, making fun of IT Industry, bosses, salaries and so on. After a long back and forth with YouTube, I stopped chasing them to get the video removed.

3. A woman I know is facing a divorce, because her information about her affair was shared with her husband by a popular search engine

4. Height of exploitation - Please go through this video http://www.youtube.com/watch?v=Z0LZ6DNCgrY, and do some research before you enter the world of web.

5. Almost everyone I know uses Facebook. A page worth visiting - https://www.facebook.com/media/set/?set=a.121633663951.103337.121628158951&type=1

6. It is estimated that at least 30% of all computers are infected with malware.

7. **Ignorance can be Suicidal** - Working on web hacking has another issue associated with awareness. The laws governing the Cyber Space are relatively new and lack of awareness has further added to confusion. There have been cases, where the lack in awareness led to extreme. Whenever in doubt, check the law before proceeding. Some real life incidents include -

A person working for Apple shared something casually, for a not so significant product. He could not bear the consequences of the treatment he received and eventually committed suicide.

When in doubt, either -

Check the legal aspects

Check the authenticity of website url before visiting the site - http://onlinelinkscan.com

References

https://thehackernews.com/search/label/Vulnerability

https://www.darknet.org.uk/

https://en.wikipedia.org/wiki/Dark_web

https://en.wikipedia.org/wiki/ECHELON

https://www.csoonline.com/article/2117843/what-is-phishing-how-this-cyber-attack-works-and-how-to-prevent-it.html

https://blog.malwarebytes.com/cybercrime/2018/08/under-the-hoodie-why-money-power-and-ego-drive-hackers-to-cybercrime/

https://cybersecurityventures.com/cybercrime-damages-6-trillion-by-2021/ b

https://www.thirdway.org/report/to-catch-a-hacker-toward-a-comprehensive-strategy-to-identify-pursue-and-punish-malicious-cyber-actors

https://www.wired.com/2017/05/silk-road-creators-life-sentence-actually-boosted-dark-web-drug-sales/

https://www.oxygen.com/crime-time/ross-ulbricht-silk-road-darknet-dream-market-wall-street

https://www.investopedia.com/terms/s/silk-road.asp

https://www.techrepublic.com/article/dark-web-the-smart-persons-guide/?ftag=CMG-01-10aaa1b

https://www.hackerone.com/blog/resources-for-new-hackers

https://hackingresources.com/

https://awesomeopensource.com/project/vitalysim/Awesome-Hacking-Resources

https://www.zdnet.com/article/failed-student-jailed-for-silk-road-dark-web-drug-profiteering/

https://www.iacpcybercenter.org/resources-2/cybercrime-community-resources/

https://1800victims.org/crime-type/cybercrimes/

https://www.unodc.org/e4j/en/cybercrime/module-5/key-issues/reporting-cybercrime.html

https://www.digitalshadows.com/blog-and-research/dark-web-monitoring-the-good-the-bad-and-the-ugly/

https://www.itseducation.asia/deep-web.htm

https://danielmiessler.com/study/internet-deep-dark-web/

https://www.webroot.com/blog/2019/07/23/out-from-the-shadows-the-dark-web/

https://cybersecurity.att.com/blogs/security-essentials/deep-web-and-dark-web

https://www.sans.org/security-awareness-training/resources/dark-web

https://www.lifelock.com/learn-identity-theft-resources-what-is-the-dark-web.html

http://people.hws.edu/hunter/deepwebgate03.htm

https://usa.kaspersky.com/resource-center/threats/deep-web

http://deep-web.org/

https://www.recordedfuture.com/dark-web-reality/

https://www.alphr.com/technology/1002667/how-to-access-the-dark-web-what-is-tor-and-how-do-i-use-it

https://www.llrx.com/2019/01/deep-web-research-and-discovery-resources-2019/?__cf_chl_jschl_tk__=73879559655e95431275590f4f19b1650f576eee-1590345538-0-AWZ5-MZEggQh09XHXadUR0_LY3iQJNfyd9v-XDICSVOXhAjUa2rECJuYfw4J9tqESHUABSkaKqegHkDwN9ECJGzksqizvNwwZaqAUoz9mX8VQo9TL0bg4lH8G56gYHOir_0riUTSEcZZPYMF-SEocWLZvsMiFq-D7xLpd-E3zD2odbeMsFaljFcan6NxwmTEEIQ0GDrFeGrEdndELNN8FaA5Ylrc3-HOHfwsezlXcxWlAphQRCxSgX58cSzJao1yO_u40AvbiO3S0AZz25lSgYR7PL5KmHYcorHzaZ69l0XLH3TFw6Te116bvJKhMKgcPom4ollDGHSf2ePa1xtwPAWUUUw6q0OvGOjV5Mm3DKfe

https://www.fraud-magazine.com/cover-article.aspx?id=4295009061

https://www.imf.org/external/pubs/ft/fandd/2019/09/the-truth-about-the-dark-web-kumar.htm

https://www.csoonline.com/article/2133495/attack-on-telenor-was-part-of-large-cyberespionage-operation-with-indian-origins-.html

Why I wrote this Book

There are books available on:

1. Penetration Testing
2. Programming to create hacking utilities
3. Beginner guides that have either just the theory or hacks that are old and no longer work
4. Books for beginners without step by step instructions

The above-mentioned points do not adequately cover the complete ecosystem of cybercrime, hacking, and espionage.

This book will:

1. Help layman to understand the entire landscape of hacking and cyber crime
2. Beginners will be able to use step by step instructions to do hacking while staying safe
3. Legal experts will be able to understand the broader landscape of cybercrime and hacking and how it impacts judiciary
4. Beginner testers will be able to take baby steps in case they want to explore the world of Penetration Testing.

Other Publications --

Published Books, Papers, and References -

Building Automated Test Systems - http://bit.ly/1nC2w7F

Silicon India - http://bit.ly/1s2ETuI

Sticky Minds - http://bit.ly/1uFghvZ

Testing Recipes - http://bit.ly/1rNIoHt

Work in Progress -

Bringing Intelligence in Search Automation - The research is in progress with a skeletal framework in place. The project is about incorporating automation to replace manual efforts by equally intelligent scripts.

The goal is to achieve increased coverage across multiple platforms, without using any commercial tool.

About the Author

Abhinav is an IT professional and has spent 18 years in the Industry working for various blue chip companies including Motorola, McAfee, Lotus Interworks, and Arctern. Some of the key products he has released include Java cross compiler Tool Chains for MIPS, Code Warrior Tool Chains, McAfee GSE, and ConsolVMS. He is Foundation member of ISTQB Indian Board and an associate of Computer Society of India. He is the author of "Search Engine Testing" and has been writing for various Technical and Research Journals.

Disclaimer

The entire text in the current book comes out of author's own research and study. The work has nothing to do with his current and/or previous employers. He has the permission of his current employer to get the work published. The references to the Public domain are cited under references section.

The findings in the current book are author's own interpretation of Cyber Security and hacking. This by any means is not intended to challenge any existing standards. Use it as per your judgment and understanding as the results can vary based on variety of reasons. The author and the publisher may not be held accountable for any damage caused due to the findings reported in the book.

Copyright

Feedback and Support - Any Technical questions, doubts, feedbacks, and scope of improvements should be addressed to the author. Unless there is high level of complexities, all queries will get addressed within one business day.

Live Webinar Events: In case the readers want a live demonstration of the work reported in the current book, please feel free to contact the author along with expectations, time zone, and preferred date to host the event.

abhinav@indiantestingboard.com

Acknowledgements

This book would not have been published without the support of multiple people me reach this stage. A note of thanks to Vivek Sharma Consultant TCS for review and creating screen captures. My special thanks to Ghiridharan Surendaran SVP, FactSet for his review and approval.

Personal Note to Readers -

###

Why I wrote this book?

During early days of my career, my computer got infected with a virus. I called up a friend who was a geek in networking and security. He came with a cd disk with an anti virus subscription for 1 year. He installed the anti-virus in my computer and cleaned the virus'es. He told me either to extend the subscription before it expires or un-install the anti-virus immediately before currently subscription expires. I eventually did not do that. To my surprise, the infections cropped up immediately after the subscription was over. However, I worked in 2 world class Security Companies and did not see any fishy activity. Its primarily not so famous companies that do it extensively. However, my security testing continued regardless of whether I was working for a Security firm or not. I have played with many virus'es, trojans, and have researched a lot on this topic. I always felt that there should be a crisp and concise compilation for general users, and not just techies, which briefs them about overall landscape of Cyber Security, hacking and espionage. That's when I started writing this book and really hope you will enjoy it. Thank you for investing valuable time reading the book. In case you need any help, any clarifications on the information presented, please feel free to get in touch.

Abhinav Vaid

Abhinav Vaid – Author
###################

Contact me –
abhinav@indiantestingboard.com
Skype – abhinavvaid

Other Coordinates -

1. Author Blog - https://testingrecipes.in/blog/
2. Facebook – https://www.facebook.com/vaidabhinav/
3. Linkedin - https://www.linkedin.com/in/abhinavvaid/

----------------------END OF BOOK--------------------